Marketing Analytics: Is Business, Digital, Marketing and 'Social Analytics' Disrupting Intellectual Property – Copyright?

Thesis · June 2016

DOI: 10.13140/RG.2.1.4325.5927

1 author:

Mohammed Nadeem

National University (California)

28 PUBLICATIONS   **52** CITATIONS

Update [summer 2016]

Marketing Analytics:

Is Business, Digital, Marketing and 'Social Analytics' Disrupting Intellectual Property - Copyright?

*Mohammed Nadeem, Ph.D.

Distinguished Professor of Marketing, National University, CA, USA.

mnadeem@nu.edu

IP Analytics

At the end of December 2002, I published my doctoral dissertation on *'The Impact of e-Commerce on Intellectual Property'* restricted to copyright from a marketing analytics perspective. At that time, Social Media websites such as *Twitter, Facebook, Pinterest, and Instagram* were non-existent. As we understand from the World Intellectual Property Organization (WIPO), "Copyright (or author's right) is a legal term used to describe the rights that creators have over their literary and artistic works. Works covered by copyright range from books, music, paintings, sculpture, and films, to computer programs, databases, advertisements, maps, and technical drawings" (WIPO, 2016).

Over the past 13 years (2002 to 2015) *much has changed* in the world of E-Commerce and Intellectual Property with the rise of Social Media particularly in the areas of *publishing, music, movies, video games, and broadcasting* from a new marketing 'social analytics' perspective.

Every April 26, we celebrate World Intellectual Property Day to learn about the role that intellectual property rights (patents, trademarks, industrial designs, copyright) play in encouraging innovation and creativity. This year, 2016, we are exploring the *future of culture in the digital age*: how we create it, how we access it, how we finance it. We are also examining how a balanced and flexible intellectual property system helps ensure that those working in the creative sector and artists themselves are properly paid for their work, so they can keep creating (WIPO, 2016).

The science of analysis using data to understand historical patterns with an eye to improving performance and predicting the future. The analysis of *digital* data refers to information collected in interactive channels *(online, mobile, social, etc.)*. Digital Analytics "has become an integral part of core business strategies and maintaining a competitive edge. Digital data started the Big Data meme as it heralded the onslaught of *Volume, Variety and Velocity*, opening the door to new types of correlative discovery much wider. Digital Analytics is a moving target of innovation and exploration. That's what makes it fascinating" (DDA, 2016).

The American Legislative Exchange Council says that "the Intellectual Property Rights (IPR) are vital to the global economy. IPR make it possible for creators to have exclusive rights to their tangible and intangible inventions, and for companies to brand their products, thus differentiating them from similar goods. Strong IPR protections also incentivize the capital-intensive research responsible for the innovations that allow human beings to live longer, healthier and happier lives. Today – at the precipice of the next industrial age hallmarked by automation, deep-data analytics and Internet-connected devices – is a great time to celebrate the role of IPR in shaping the future" (Thompson, 2016).

Two related trends characterize the recent past: value propositions are migrating from the physical to the informational, and value creation is shifting from firms to consumers. These two trends meet in the phenomenon of "consumer-generated intellectual property" (CGIP). A recent research (Berthon, Pitt, Kietzmann & McCarthy, 2015) study addresses the question: "How should firms manage the intellectual property that their customers create?" It explored how CGIP presents important dilemmas for managers and argues that consumers' "intellectual property" should not be leveraged at the expense of their "emotional property." The study integrated these perspectives into a diagnostic framework and discusses eight strategies for firms to manage CGIP".

Moreover, the systematic integrated management of intellectual property (IP) is a recent phenomenon. This is despite the fact that intellectual property has been around for several centuries. Today, matters are more complicated, and integrated IP management is required. By integrated IP management meant not only that the various forms of intellectual property (patents, trade secrets, trademarks, copyright) are managed together, but that intellectual property management is in turn integrated with overall business model design and corporate strategy. Integrated management is more than simply establishing a licensing model, or manufacturing a product that incorporates new invention (Al-Aali, & Teece, 2013).

In many organizations, the research & development, strategy, and legal functions continue to be poorly integrated. As a consequence, firms miss opportunities to create and exploit the value of intellectual property. Functional silos are one reason for the lack of integration. More important, however, is the lack of a common framework and even language that would allow engineers, lawyers, and business executives to manage IP assets better. Fisher III, & Oberholzer-Gee (2013) study argued that "there is no one best way to manage IP and many managers overestimate the attractiveness of using IP to exert market power. Rather, the value of the various means to protect and benefit from IP depends on firm strategy, the competitive landscape, and the rapidly changing contours of intellectual property law".

Over the years, the licensing of intellectual property (IP) has been growing dramatically. A distinguishing feature of licensing versus standard sales is that license contracts often involve self-reporting; the licensor relies on the licensee to report the royalties owed. Autrey, & Sansing, (2014) in a recent study examined "self-reporting licensing contracts using a game-theoretic approach to royalty compliance. A licensee's accounting system generates a potentially inaccurate royalty report provided to the licensor. This self-reporting gives rise to demand for auditing by the licensor. The authors characterized the optimal royalty contract, accounting system choice by the licensee, and audit strategy choice by the licensor. The authors find that self-reporting either (a) limits the licensee's rents, but lowers social welfare, or (b) enhances social welfare by facilitating use of the IP by the low-cost licensee instead of the high-cost licensor. As accounting system costs decrease or the gains from outsourcing increase, variable royalties based on self-reporting become even more desirable".

E-Commerce & Marketing Analytics

E-Commerce as we understand is the application of information and communications technology from the point of customer's login to the point of customer's receiving the goods along electronically with manually processing system. The Internet potential for electronic commerce was expected to boom with the spread of the Internet but, the lack of consumer confidence in electronic payments as regards security of payment mechanisms explained the slow growth of online purchase. Thus, in a study (Akazue, & Augusta, 2015) argued that "a centralized merchant registration retrieval (CMRR) component of e-commerce model is used to serve as an advisory tool that identify cloned payment page in e-commerce transaction. An online evaluation of the use of CMRR in identifying cloned payment page and acting as an advisory to customer were carried out through the use of questionnaire. Data analysis of generated questionnaire showed that CMRR can enhance customer's confidence and trust in the purchase of online goods and services via identifying cloned payment page".

What factors underlie the adoption dynamics of ecommerce technologies among users in developing countries? Even though the internet promised to be the great equalizer, the nuanced variety of conditions and contingencies that shape user adoption of ecommerce technologies has received little scrutiny. Building on previous research on technology adoption, Datta (2011) proposed "a global information technology (IT) adoption model. The model includes antecedents of performance expectancy, social influence, and technology opportunism and investigates the crucial influence of facilitating conditions. The proposed model is tested using data from 172 technology users from 37 countries, collected over a 1-year period. The findings suggest that in developing countries, facilitating conditions play a critical moderating role in understanding actual ecommerce adoption, especially when in tandem with technological opportunism. Altogether, the study offered a preliminary scrutiny of the mechanics of ecommerce adoption in developing countries".

Using both primary and secondary research, a research study (Fleet, 2012) sought to "underline the role of facilitators in the progressive evolution and adoption of e-commerce and eBusiness among SMEs. In particular, the study examined the role of Internet marketing as the trigger for successful facilitation of, and evolution to, richer eBusiness services". An earlier Atlantic Canadian study by Davies & Vladica (2004) introduced "the notion of facilitators as the key to moving SMEs along a progressive adoption of ICT and eBusiness services". A more recent UK study (Gray, 2009), theorizes on the "tremendous challenges SMEs face in e-commerce adoption, specifically with the step from having a basic web site to transacting with goods and services online. The implications for understanding and assisting SMEs is obvious; as well, policy makers can now focus their policy and program efforts beyond infrastructure building to training in services that can help SMEs overcome barriers in adoption and move up the e-commerce adoption path".

Although extremely popular, E-Commerce environments often lack information that has traditionally served to ensure trust among exchange partners. Digital technologies, however, have created new forms of 'electronic word-of-mouth,' which offer new potential for gathering credible information that guides consumer behaviors. A recent research (Flanagin et al., 2014) study conducted "a nationally representative survey and a focused experiment to assess how individuals perceive the credibility of online commercial information, particularly as compared to information available through more traditional channels, and to evaluate the specific aspects of ratings information that affect people's attitudes toward ecommerce. Survey results show that consumers rely heavily on web-based information as compared to other channels, and that ratings information is critical in the evaluation of the credibility of online commercial information. Experimental results indicate that ratings are positively associated with perceptions of product quality and purchase intention, but that people attend to average product ratings, but not to the number of ratings or to the combination of the average and the number of ratings together. Thus suggests that in spite of valuing the web and ratings as sources of commercial information, people use ratings information sub-optimally by potentially privileging small numbers of ratings that could be idiosyncratic. In addition, product quality is shown to mediate the relationship between user ratings and purchase intention".

Concerns of potential online consumers over privacy and security of their financial and other personal information is an impediment to the growth of ecommerce. These concerns are often addressed through the use of assurance structures placed on a website. Prior research has found that the effect of assurance structures is most pronounced when the vendor is unknown to the consumer and they have no prior interactions from which to judge the trustworthiness of the vendor. Another important factor to decision making under uncertainty in any context is the perceived problem domain of the decision maker. Behavioral Decision Theory helps to explain the behavior of individuals in decisions under uncertainty in terms of the perceived problem domain. Prospect Theory (Kahneman and Tversky, 1979) was used in a recent research study (Bahmanziari, & Odom (2015) to attempt to explain "variance in the behavior of individuals under conditions of uncertainty in the ecommerce context. A major proposition in this study was that since consumers are risk-averse in the gain domain; the risk relieving properties of assurance structures may moderate their decisions and induce more trust and purchase intentions and behavior. However, in the perceived loss domain, where risk- seeking behavior is common, little to no effect was expected since the reduction of risk is not a driving factor of the purchase decision. The study was a 2 x 2 fully crossed factorial design. Two factors, problem domain and the presence of assurance structures were manipulated with a dependent variable of purchase behavior. Subjects for this study were solicited from undergraduate students enrolled in accounting and management classes at a large Midwestern university. A total of 400 subjects participated in the study with 337 usable responses. The data provided the first evidence of framing effects in the ecommerce environment. The study also demonstrated that assurance structures moderate choice shifts attributed to the framing effect in the ecommerce environment".

A rapidly growing number of marketers consider virtual worlds a compelling opportunity to reach and interact with current and potential consumers. These marketers face complex challenges, many of them brought about by the unique nature of an economy comprised of real dollars being used to acquire virtual products. Bonifiled & Tomas (2009) study explored one challenge these marketers face: "protection of their intellectual property in the virtual world".

Small and Medium Enterprises (SMEs) continue to struggle to measure the success of their website. This results in ineffective eCommerce activities and the consequent disappointment in recognizable benefits. There is a need for a website operational model offering managers the ability to understand the payoffs from their investment. Ghandour (2015) study presented "an empirically proven intuitive eCommerce website operational model that offers managers a comprehensive way of understanding their website operation. The model premise is simple: the achievement of operational excellence will lead to improved financial performance. The central task for managers, then, lies in understanding what drives operational excellence and then committing the necessary resources to the development of the drivers".

Social Media Analytics

Online social casinos and real-money gambling industries, including gambling at online and live venues (such as casino resorts), are quickly converging (H2 Gambling Capital & Odobo, 2013). Abarbanel & Rahman (2015) study argued "using data collected from 339 online real money gamblers, the relationship between player demographics and gambling preferences and frequency of online social casino participation is examined. Frequency of play in social casino games varied depending on gender and education, similar to patterns in real money gambling. Players who participated more frequently in social casino games were also more likely to spend more time participating in real money online gambling. Findings provide consumer insight for online gambling and social casino companies working toward convergence of the two game types, including implications for target markets for crossover play, loyalty programs, and corporate social responsibility".

Of all the challenges which face business, the discovery, exploitation, retention and protection of intellectual property have been identified as the most serious within the context of small high technology firms and restricts the scope to technology-related intellectual property (IP), the marketing competencies necessary for successful IP marketing. Rod, & Paliwoda (2015) study argued following a review of the relevant literature, the question that arises is "whether mainstream marketing principles are sufficient to service the needs of technology enabled but resource limited SMEs or whether the adoption of entrepreneurial marketing is more appropriate"?

We know the importance of knowledge management for the development of organizations, regions and countries and the need for protecting the same by intellectual property laws when transformed from intangible to tangible assets. Manuel (2016) studied the "link between Knowledge Management (KM) and Intellectual Property (IP). The paper begins with the history of both subjects and ends by studying the linkage between these subjects. The study concludes that countries with weak protection of IPR should develop measures for promoting protection of IP, as well as allow technological development and encourage marketing, inventions and innovations. They must be accompanied by measures to promote the increase of human capital so that they can identify market opportunities and promote a culture of innovation".

Messer, Butler & Tsan (2016) study discussed use of social media in civil cases and need for businesses to evaluate their interact on social media. It mentions "use of social media discovery in litigations including jurisdiction, intellectual property and employment. It adds the case Congregation Rabbinical College of Tartikov, Inc. v. Village of Pomona in which Village Trustee made and deleted a Facebook post that resulted in sanctions against the Village and case Allied Concrete Co. v. Lester on same".

Gautam (2014) study argued that "social media has become increasingly necessary for staying connected in our globalized and tech-savvy society. Although social media has become a staple of modern life and a regular part of business, the legal definition of social media remains undefined. State legislatures have remained silent on the topic, but as business and individual account holders find themselves seeking bankruptcy relief, it becomes clear that treatment under the Bankruptcy Code depends on definitions that do not yet exist. The question of how social media should be characterized leaves bankruptcy courts uncertain as to whether social media accounts should be included in the bankruptcy estate. While social media encompasses aspects of property, intellectual property, and other rights, this Comment argues that social media does not fit solely into any of these categories. Instead, this Comment argues for the classification of a social media account as more similar to a personal privilege than a traditional property right. The study concludes that state legislatures should legally define social media to foster predictability of its role especially in bankruptcy proceedings".

Mitchell (2014) study discussed a proposed "framework for addressing individuals' legal rights to social media contact lists, focusing on U.S. intellectual property and trade secrets laws, as well as information about the legal aspects of various social networking services such as Facebook, Twitter, and LinkedIn. American copyright and patent laws are mentioned, along with fiduciary duties and a patent law-related shop-right rule in America. The study examined Social media profiles and several legal cases".

Rustad & Koenig (2014) study offered information on "the significant need for legal reform to contract formation practices of the social media websites regarding their terms of use (TOU) and privacy policy under the intellectual property law of the U.S. It informs that the social network provider Instatgram filed a consumer arbitration proceeding with the American Arbitration Association (AAA) regarding the Seventh Amendment right to a jury trial and liberal discovery".

Copyright – Social Analytics

A US Business Law and Tax Expert, Murray (2016), explained that "social media such as *Twitter, Facebook, and Pinterest*, allow online posting of material that may be copyrighted. The social media site does not own the work that has been posted on their site; the copyright is still retained by the owner/consumer. However by agreeing to post works on the site, the owner/consumer signs an agreement that gives the site a license to use the work. In these cases, the license is given without payment".

Twitter and Copyright

The Twitter Terms of Service state (Murray, 2016) that "the owner/consumer retains the rights to any content submitted, posted or displayed on or through the Services. By submitting, posting or displaying content on or through the services, the owner/consumer grants twitter a worldwide, non-exclusive, royalty-free license (with the right to sublicense) to use, copy, reproduce, process, adapt, modify, publish, transmit, display and distribute such content in any and all media or distribution methods (now known or later developed). In other words, Twitter users grant Twitter a license to make Tweets available to other Twitter users".

Facebook and Copyright

The Facebook Terms are similar, stating that (Murray, 2016) the Facebook user own "all of the content and information posted on Facebook, and the owner/consumer can control how it is shared through its privacy and application settings." In addition, for content protected by intellectual property rights, the owner/consumer grants Facebook a non-exclusive, transferable, sub-licensable, royalty-free, worldwide license to use any IP content that is posted on or in connection with Facebook (IP License). When owner/consumer leaves Facebook, all content is deleted".

Pinterest and Copyright

Pinterest is a social media site that allows members to post photos from their websites and other places. Pinterest's terms of service says that (Muarry, 2016) Pinterest "does not take owner/consumer copyright to photos. However, by signing up for Pinterest and agreeing to their terms and privacy notice, the owner/consumer have agreed to give Pinterest a non-exclusive, royalty-free, transferable, sub-licensable, worldwide license to use, display, reproduce, re-pin, modify (e.g., re-format), re-arrange, and distribute owner/consumers User Content on Pinterest for the purposes of operating and providing the Service(s) to the owner/consumer and to its other Users. In other words, Pinterest can use the owner/consumer content on its site because the owner/consumer have agreed to give Pinterest a license to use it as described in this agreement, without payment. The Pinterest copyright statement includes a link where the owner/consumer can file a complaint against someone the owner/consumer feel has violated copyright".

Protecting Owner/Consumer Content on Social Media

Finally Murray (2016) also emphasized that "the best way to protect our intellectual property from being appropriated on social media is to not to post/share in the first place. Although the owner/consumer owns the content placed on one of these social media sites, the owner/consumer have granted a license to the media site to use the content and for others to view it. To protect content, includes a copyright statement on the file for photos. Moreover the owner/consumer property might get appropriated by someone (not associated with the social media site). The owner/consumer be vigilant to keep track of possible violations and be quick to file complaints and if necessary to support claims in a lawsuit".

IP's Future - Discussion Analytics

In business environment, it is argued that modularity is a means of partitioning technical knowledge about a product or process. When state-sanctioned IP rights are ineffective or costly to enforce, modularity can be used to hide information and thus protect IP. Baldwin, & Henkel, (2015) examined "the impact of modularity on IP protection by formally modeling the threat of expropriation by agents. The principal had three options to address this threat: trust, licensing, and paying agents to stay loyal. The study showed how the principal can influence the value of these options by modularizing the system and by hiring clans of agents, thus exploiting relationships among them. Extensions address screening and signaling in hiring, the effects of an imperfect legal system, and social norms of fairness".

Case in Point 1: The Tobacco Plain Packaging Act (TPPA) was passed in Australia in 2011 and set restrictions on the appearance of tobacco packages. The restrictions limited the use of trademarks to only the brand name, and banned any use of distinctive colors or images. Tobacco growing nations believed this restriction on trade dress violated Article 20 of the Trade-Related Aspects of Intellectual Property Rights (TRIPS) Agreement, which guarantees that no restriction may unjustifiably encumber intellectual property. Article 8 of the TRIPS Agreement, however, allows for encumbrances when it is intended to promote the protection of public health and safety. The tobacco growing nations brought a complaint to the World Trade Organization (WTO), alleging the TPPA violated the TRIPS Agreement. Lease (2016) Note "analyzed the WTO case law to determine whether the tobacco growing countries will succeed on their claim, or if Australia may successfully argue the TRIPS Article 8 health exception allows the restriction. The Note also discusses the purpose of the WTO--whether the WTO is the best mediator between a government's right to implement health-based restrictions and an intellectual property holder's guaranteed right of freedom from restrictions, and the potential ramifications of the WTO's decision. The Note concluded that the TPPA is an unjustifiable encumbrance under the TRIPS Agreement and that the WTO's Dispute Settlement Panel should find the TPPA violates the TRIPS Agreement".

In addition, a study by Steensma, Chari, & Heidl (2015) argued that "expansive patent portfolios may be used by firms to fence off technological space for commercialization, impede the commercialization efforts of competitors, and enhance bargaining power in cross-licensing negotiations. Low quality patents with claims that overlap those of other patents contribute to these portfolios and patent strategies. By failing to disclose known relevant prior art during the patenting process, inventors and their firms may be granted low quality patents with intellectual property claims which would not otherwise have been granted. We find that the failure of inventors to disclose known relevant prior art increases as they gain experience with the patenting process. Such failure is also greater among inventors employed by relatively small, poorly performing firms that rely on outsourced legal counsel during the application process".

Case in Point 2: The biopharmaceutical research and development is overwhelmingly focused in the U.S. because it is incentivized and encouraged through a robust intellectual property rights protection environment. Across the board, the United States provides the most comprehensive, effective intellectual property rights protections for biopharmaceuticals. As a result, the industry locates researches and thrives in the US. With an acknowledgement of the importance of intellectual property rights as well as the wider benefits of biopharmaceutical research and development, it's tremendously disappointing that the recently negotiated Trans-Pacific Partnership (TPP) Trade Agreement fails to deliver sufficient IP protection for biologics. Lybecker (2016) study explored "the importance of a rigorous intellectual property environment for the biopharmaceutical industry through an examination of the importance of data exclusivity provisions. Such protection is critical as the number, complexity and cost of clinical trials increases. Technology inevitably evolves faster than the legal architecture that surrounds it. As technology evolves, making the development of new biologic vaccines and therapies possible, society's commitment to incentivize innovation and protect it must be enshrined in the intellectual property protections of agreements such as the TPP".

Given recent developments in information technology and intellectual property (IP) legislation, technology firms may likely to benefit from an integrated IP strategy that combines patenting with strategic disclosure. Peters, Thiel, & Tucci (2013) study presented "a series of cases that introduced various aspects of strategic disclosure and provide a framework for how and when such practices may be merited as part of an integrated IP strategy. To help CEOs decide on the economics and efficiency of the practice, practical guidelines are provided for when it might be a useful complement to the firm's other IP management practices".

Conley, Bican, & Ernst (2013) study emphasized that:

"innovative companies are increasingly moving beyond the legal-oriented and patent-focused IP departments of the past to adopt a more strategic and cross-functional approach to IP management. As Ed Schummer, former licensing Vice President of Dolby Laboratories, describes it: "While the Dolby intellectual property was the foundation of the licensing business, it took a committed focus on the customer to build the trust and the relationships that in the end drove revenue. This was a cross-functional activity that included engineers and market savvy professionals working closely with both device and content producers. The resulting customer equity and brand recognition helped Dolby move through at least two major focus transitions." 66 This change is in line with the core managerial message of the value articulation framework, Fig. 1:

FIGURE 1. The Value Articulation Framework that connects IPR Management with Market Opportunities[8]

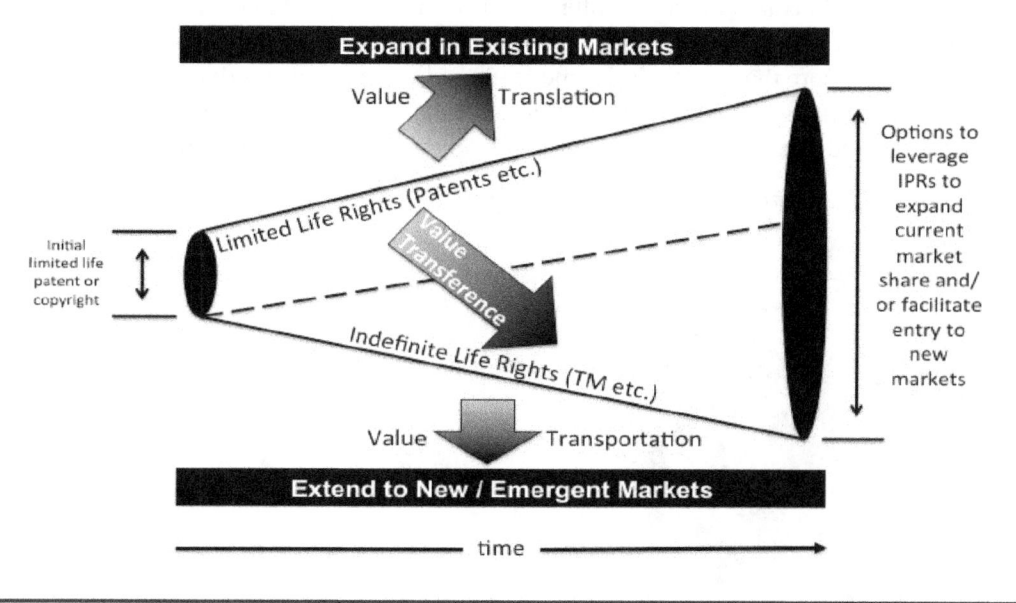

Source: Conley, J. G., Bican, P. M., & Ernst, H. (2013). Value Articulation: A FRAMEWORK FOR THE STRATEGIC MANAGEMENT OF INTELLECTUAL PROPERTY. *California Management Review*, 55(4), 102-120.

It brings the discussion of IP out of the clouds of technology and law down into the heart of marketing, new product development, and strategy. The patent-centric view of IP neglects the strategic importance of leveraging the various IP regimes over time. The value articulation framework offers a view on who should be actively involved in the process of defining and executing transference, translation, and transportation. Given recent billion dollar IP transactions,67 the returns to be realized from IP options are self-evident. With the framework, entrepreneurs, managers, and academics can gain insight into how the optionality embedded in IPR regimes can build and sustain competitive advantage. The value articulation framework connects IP options, investments, and benefits in a unique way to enable growth in existing markets and to lead the transition to new markets".

Technological innovation drives long-term economic growth, so most countries attempt to provide an innovation-friendly environment that includes tightening protection of intellectual property rights (IPR). However, debate continues on whether strengthened IPR lead to technological development and economic growth: patents promote innovation by protecting appropriation from invention and disclosing knowledge to the public, but they also create excessive monopoly power that may impede further innovation. Using simultaneous equations with cross-country panel data from 12 countries and 3 industries (chemical, electronic, machinery), Woo, Jang, & Kim (2015) study "estimated the direct effect of IPR on industry value added and the indirect effect of it through enhanced research and development (R&D). The bilateral role of IPR, as measured by patented knowledge, was used to distinguish different characteristics of industries as well as the positive and negative effects of IPR on innovation. Results suggest that IPR generally enhance industry value added, but the positive effect is mitigated with increased enforcement of IPR. Also, IPR enhanced R&D but showed a negative relationship with patented knowledge, suggesting that excessive propertization of knowledge may hinder sequential innovation. The positive role of IPR on R&D predominated in the chemical (discrete) industry and exerted negative effects in the electronic and machinery (complex) industries".

Thompson (2016) study illustrated how important IP-intensive sectors are to the U.S. economy: "The latest Global Intellectual Property Center IP index reports that IP-intensive industries employ 40 million Americans and pay wages that average 30 percent more than other industries. These workers produce 72.5 percent more than the typical American worker, and their products account for 74 percent of all exports. The latest filing statistics from the United Nations' World Intellectual Property Organization (WIPO) on patents and trademarks make clear how international competition in IP drives innovation.

2015 PCT Applicants by Field

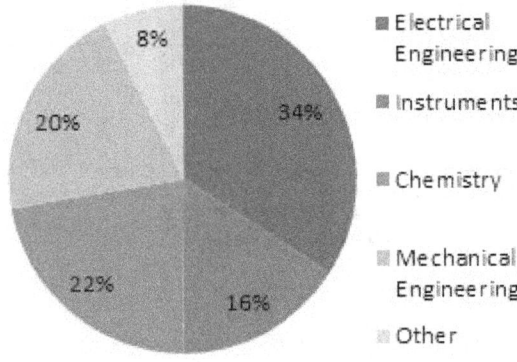

Figure: 2 Adapted from 2016 WIPO Statistical Filings

2015 Top 10 PCT Patent Applicants

1. Huawei Technologies (China)

2. Qualcomm (USA)

3. ZTE (China)

4. Samsung (Rep. of Korea)

5. Mitsubishi (Japan)

6. Ericsson (Sweden)

7. LG Electronics (Rep. of Korea)

8. Sony Corp (Japan)

9. Philips (Netherlands)

10. Hewlett-Packard (USA)

Table 1: World Intellectual Property Organization 2016 Statistical Filings".

Thompson (2016) also highlighted that:

"The fields that filed the most patents in 2015 were electrical machinery and digital communication in the electrical engineering field. These fields filed fewer applications than the year before, but continue to occupy the largest portion of the total share of applications – 7.3 and 8 percent respectively. However, Asia continues to grow its share of world inventions. China, the Republic of Korea and Japan filed 42 percent of PCT applications in 2015 with China alone increasing its applications by 9 percent. Universities contribute significantly to the pool of patent applications. Thanks to the 1980 Bayh-Dole Act that allows U.S. universities to own and license inventions created with federal research funding, U.S. universities patent more inventions than their global peers and account for 50 percent of all educational institution applications in the world.

2015 Top Ten PCT Patent Applications from Educational Institutions

University of California (USA)	361	University of Michigan (USA)	116
Massachusetts Institute of Technology (USA)	213	University of Florida (USA)	108
Johns Hopkins University (USA)	170	Tsinghua University (China)	102
University of Texas (USA)	163	University of Tokyo (Japan)	101
Harvard University (USA)	158	Leland Stanford Junior University (USA)	99

Table 2: World Intellectual Property Organization 2016 Statistical Filings

Without strong protections for IPR, creators lack the incentive to invest in new innovations, and corporations are discouraged from expanding into new markets. It is in everyone's best interest to protect the IPR that spur the innovation economy and enhance quality of life".

Perhaps the future of any IP analytics including---*business, digital, marketing and social*---is not only a perspective but also predictive!

References:

1. Abarbanel, B., & Rahman, A. (2015). eCommerce Market Convergence in Action: Social Casinos and Real Money Gambling. UNLV Gaming Research & Review Journal, 19(1), 51-62.
2. Al-Aali, A. Y., & Teece, D. J. (2013). Towards the (Strategic) Management of Intellectual Property: RETROSPECTIVE AND PROSPECTIVE. California Management Review, 55(4), 15-30. doi:10.1525/cmr.2013.55.4.15.
3. Akazue, M., & Augusta, A. (2015). Identification of Cloned Payment Page in Ecommerce Transaction. International Management Review, 11(2), 70-76.
4. Autrey, R. L., & Sansing, R. (2014). Licensing Intellectual Property With Self-Reported Outcomes. Journal Of Accounting, Auditing & Finance, 29(3), 260-277. doi:10.1177/0148558X14530130.
5. Baldwin, C. Y., & Henkel, J. (2015). Modularity and intellectual property protection. Strategic Management Journal, 36(11), 1637-1655. doi:10.1002/smj.2303.
6. Bahmanziari, T., & Odom, M. D. (2015). PROSPECT THEORY AND RISKY CHOICE IN THE ECOMMERCE SETTING: EVIDENCE OF A FRAMING EFFECT. Academy Of Accounting & Financial Studies Journal, 19(1), 85-106.
7. Berthon, P., Pitt, L., Kietzmann, J., & McCarthy, I. P. (2015). CGIP: MANAGING CONSUMER-GENERATED INTELLECTUAL PROPERTY. *California Management Review*, *57*(4), 43-62. doi:10.1525/cmr.2015.57.4.43.
8. Bonifield, C. M., & Tomas, A. M. (2009). Intellectual property issues for marketers in the virtual world. Journal Of Brand Management,16(8), 571-581. doi:10.1057/bm.2008.41.
9. Conley, J. G., Bican, P. M., & Ernst, H. (2013). Value Articulation: A FRAMEWORK FOR THE STRATEGIC MANAGEMENT OF INTELLECTUAL PROPERTY. California Management Review, 55(4), 102-120. doi:10.1525/cmr.2013.55.4.102..
10. Datta, P. (2011). A preliminary study of ecommerce adoption in developing countries. Information Systems Journal, 21(1), 3-32. doi:10.1111/j.1365-2575.2009.00344.x.
11. Digital Analytics (2016, May 29). *Digital Analytics Association,* retrieved from http://www.digitalanalyticsassociation.org/
12. Digital Creativity (2016, May, 30). *Culture Reimagined*, retrieved from http://www.wipo.int/ip-outreach/en/ipday.
13. GAUTAM, S. (2014). #BANKRUPTCY: RECONSIDERING "PROPERTY" TO DETERMINE THE ROLE OF SOCIAL MEDIA IN THE BANKRUPTCY ESTATE. Emory Bankruptcy Developments Journal, 31(1), 127-145.
14. Ghandour, A. (2015). ECOMMERCE WEBSITE VALUE MODEL FOR SMES. International Journal Of Electronic Commerce Studies,6(2), 203-222. doi:10.7903/ijecs.1403.
15. Flanagin, A., Metzger, M., Pure, R., Markov, A., & Hartsell, E. (2014). Mitigating risk in ecommerce transactions: perceptions of information credibility and the role of user-generated ratings in product quality and purchase intention. Electronic Commerce Research, 14(1), 1-23. doi:10.1007/s10660-014-9139-2.
16. Fleet, G. J. (2012). EVIDENCE FOR STALLED ICT ADOPTION AND THE FACILITATOR ECOMMERCE ADOPTION MODEL IN SMEs. International Journal Of The Academic Business World, 6(2), 7-18.
17. Fisher III, W. W., & Oberholzer-Gee, F. (2013). Strategic Management of Intellectual Property: AN INTEGRATED APPROACH.California Management Review, 55(4), 157-183. doi:10.1525/cmr.2013.55.4.157.

18. Lease, K. (2016). SMOKE 'EM IF YOU GOT 'EM: INTELLECTUAL PROPERTY RIGHTS IN THE TOBACCO INDUSTRY GOING UP IN SMOKE. *Case Western Reserve Journal Of International Law*, 48(1/2), 371-394.

19. Lybecker, K. M. (2016). Intellectual Property Protection for Biologics: Why the Trans-Pacific Partnership (TPP) Trade Agreement Fails to Deliveri. *Journal Of Commercial Biotechnology*, 22(1), 42-48. doi:10.5912/jcb731.

20. Manuel, E. G. (2016). Knowledge Management and Intellectual Property. *IUP Journal Of Knowledge Management*, 14(1), 45-68.

21. Rod, M. M., & Paliwoda, S. J. (2015). Perspectives on SMEs and the entrepreneurial marketing of intellectual property. *International Journal Of Entrepreneurship & Innovation Management*, 19(3/4), 147-162. doi:10.1504/IJEIM.2015.069953.

22. Messer, S. M., Butler, B. J., & Tsan, C. G. (2016). E-Discovery and Information Management: Can Clicking "Like" Make or Break a Lawsuit?. *Intellectual Property & Technology Law Journal*, 28(4), 15-16.

23. Mitchell, C. J. (2014). Keep Your Friends Close: A Framework for Addressing Rights to Social Media Contacts. *Vanderbilt Law Review*, 67(5), 1459-1495.

24. Murray, J. (2016, April 25). Social Media and Copyright. Retrieved from http://biztaxlaw.about.com/od/copyrights/a/Copyrights-And-Social-Media-Issues.htm

25. Peters, T., Thiel, J., & Tucci, C. L. (2013). Protecting Growth Options in Dynamic Markets: THE ROLE OF STRATEGIC DISCLOSURE IN INTEGRATED INTELLECTUAL PROPERTY STRATEGIES. *California Management Review*, 55(4), 121-142. doi:10.1525/cmr.2013.55.4.121.

26. Rustad, M. L., & Koenig, T. H. (2014). WOLVES OF THE WORLD WIDE WEB: REFORMING SOCIAL NETWORKS' CONTRACTING PRACTICES. *Wake Forest Law Review*, 49(5), 1431-1517.

27. Thompson, P, (2016, May 25). Intellectual Property Rights Shapes The Future, retrieved from https://www.alec.org/article/intellectual-property-rights-shape-the-future/

28. Woo, S., Jang, P., & Kim, Y. (2015). Effects of intellectual property rights and patented knowledge in innovation and industry value added: A multinational empirical analysis of different industries. *Technovation*, 43/4449-63. doi:10.1016/j.technovation.2015.03.003.

Adjunct Professor of Marketing, School of Management, University of San Francisco, CA, USA.

INFORMATION TO USERS

This manuscript has been reproduced from the microfilm master. UMI films the text directly from the original or copy submitted. Thus, some thesis and dissertation copies are in typewriter face, while others may be from any type of computer printer.

The quality of this reproduction is dependent upon the quality of the copy submitted. Broken or indistinct print, colored or poor quality illustrations and photographs, print bleedthrough, substandard margins, and improper alignment can adversely affect reproduction.

In the unlikely event that the author did not send UMI a complete manuscript and there are missing pages, these will be noted. Also, if unauthorized copyright material had to be removed, a note will indicate the deletion.

Oversize materials (e.g., maps, drawings, charts) are reproduced by sectioning the original, beginning at the upper left-hand corner and continuing from left to right in equal sections with small overlaps.

The Impact of eCommerce

on Intellectual Property

Mohammed M. Nadeem

The Union Institute and University

Graduate College

Ph.D. in Interdisciplinary Studies

Area of concentration: eBusiness

December 2002

Dr. Ben Davis
First Core Faculty Advisor

UMI Number: 3074711

ProQuest Information and Learning Company
300 North Zeeb Road
P.O. Box 1346
Ann Arbor, MI 48106-1346

Abstract:

"The Impact of eCommerce on Intellectual Property"

This study addressed the impact of eCommerce on intellectual property copyright laws and regulations. eCommerce self-regulatory efforts, technological restraints and standards are undergoing legal challenges. Qualitative research methodology based on content analysis procedures confirmed the hypothesis that if legal rules are not set and applied appropriately, digital technology has the potential to undermine the basic tenets of copyright laws and regulations. The study excluded analysis of domain names, patents, and trademarks issues. The data suggested that new intellectual property products will be primarily digital and will be delivered online.

The results support the hypothesis that adjustment in the U.S. legal system be made to respond to the new technological environment in an effective and appropriate way. Conclusions addressed anti-circumvention and copyright management information, fair use, temporary copies, first sale, and pre-emption to achieve a goal of maintaining the crucial balance between ownership and access rights for successful global eCommerce transactions. Recommendations for further research cover the areas of digital millennium copyright act, the rise of digital rights management technologies, standardization and copyright levies.

Dedication

By the grace and mercy of God, I dedicate this Project Demonstrating Excellence to my wife Sarah and my children for standing by me as I spent the countless hours of time that could have been spent with them.

Acknowledgements

First, I would like to thank Dr. Ben Davis for his encouragement, guidance and support. I also want to express my appreciation to Dr. Justin Abraham, who inspired me, taught me, and kept me on my toes. And thanks to Dr. Richard Kustin for guiding me in exploring a broader theoretical perspective on eBusiness and eCommerce. His input, responsiveness, and support were crucial in bringing this study to its successful completion. I would also like to express my appreciation to my Peers Suzanne Sincavage and Joy Wolfe for their invaluable support, inspiration, and guidance from an interdisciplinary perspective.

I would also like to thank my parents for their love, infinite patience, and support. Finally, the encouragement to accomplish a major piece of work comes from friends, especially Razi MohiUddin, Chairman and CEO of IronSpeed.com (formerly Buckaroo.com). Without all of these wonderful people, this study just could not have been realized, and I am grateful to them all.

Table of Contents

<u>Title</u>		<u>Page</u>
Chapter 1: Study Overview		**8**
I.	Introduction	8
II.	Statement of the Problem	27
	A. Research Question	28
	B. Sub-Problems	29
	C. Hypothesis	31
	D. Research Methodology Statement	32
IIII.	Purpose of the Study	33
IV.	Scope and Limitations of the Study	34
V.	Chapter Summary	36
Chapter 2: Descriptive Literature Review		**38**
I.	Introduction	38
II.	Literature Review	38
III.	Groundwork	50
	A. WIPO-International Dimensions of eCommerce	50
	B. IITF 1995 Report-IP and the NII	54
	C. Hardy's 1998 Report-Future of Copyright	57
	D. National Academies Press 2000 Report-Digital Dilemma	59
	E. International Copyright Treaties and	61

the Role of the United States

F. Online Business Models   70

IV.   Chapter Summary   78

Chapter 3: Research Methodology and Data Collection   **80**

I.   Introduction   80

II.   Qualitative Research Methodology   80

    A. Phase One: Data Collection   82

    B. Phase Two: Testing Research Hypothesis   83

    C. Phase Three: Theory Construction   91

III.   Technological Protection Measures, Online Business   96

    Models and DMCA

IV.   Chapter Summary   112

Chapter 4: Analysis and Results   **115**

I.   Introduction   115

II.   Analysis and Results   115

    A. Technological Protection Measures   116

    B. Intellectual Property Implications of Traditional   121

    Business Models

    C. Intellectual Property Implications of   123

    Less Traditional Business Models

III.   Four Positions: DRM, DMCA, Fair Use, and   124

        Free Speech

IV.   Surveys   131

V.   Chapter Summary   138

Chapter 5: Interpretation, Conclusions, and   140

        Recommendations

I.   Introduction   140

II.   Review of the Problem   140

III.   Interpretation   142

IV.   Conclusions and Study's Contributions   150

V.   Recommendations for Future Research   157

VI.   Chapter Summary   164

VII.   Project Demonstrating Excellence Summary   167

Appendix A: References   170

Appendix B: Survey Consent Form   180

Chapter 1: Study Overview

I. Introduction

The purpose of this chapter is to introduce the overview of the Project Demonstrating Excellence (PDE) on the impact of electronic commerce (eCommerce) on intellectual property copyright laws and regulations. It includes statement of the problem, research question, sub-problems, hypothesis, research methodology statement, purpose, scope and limitations of the study, and chapter summary.

The world of eCommerce is undergoing a major consolidation. Most of the pure-play companies failed to come up with a viable revenue model but the fascination of consumers to buy online and to surf the web for information continues unabated. More than 100 million Americans visit the web every month and popular portals such as Yahoo and MSN continue to attract over thirty million visitors a month. The volume of sales in business-to-consumer sector continues to grow at more than 50 percent a year. This is reflected by the growing participation in e-retailing by conventional brick-and-mortar companies. WalMart, and K-Mart have launched major initiatives. Companies such as Dell and Cisco do business on the web that runs into millions of dollars a day (Chaudhury, Kuilboer, 2002).

In the 1990s, the commercialization of the Internet set off a revolution in the use of information technology for conducting business. Old assumptions about the cost structure and geographic limits of networked systems became irrelevant; it became possible to build systems with worldwide reach quickly and inexpensively. Business people responded by creating entirely new types of businesses and fundamentally altering existing businesses. The once limited strategic use of information technology became widespread. New terms were created to label this revolution: electronic commerce (more commonly called eCommerce) and electronic business (eBusiness), (McNurlin, Sprague, 2002).

The business world is transitioning from a physical reality based on atoms to a digital one of bits (Kalakota, Robinson 2001). The term commerce is viewed by some as transactions conducted between business partners. Therefore, the term eCommerce seems to be fairly narrow to some people. Thus, use the term eBusiness. It refers to a broader definition of eCommerce, not just buying and selling but also servicing customers and collaborating with business partners, and conducting electronic transactions within an organization (Turban, Lee, King, Chung, 2000).

Business-to-business eCommerce is the largest gold rush international commerce has seen for decades. It may be the largest ever (Cunningham, 2001). Bridging the profound gap between the way traditional businesses are run and the way virtual communities will be built and run represents the single greatest challenge for senior management of existing companies. Most people will need to adopt a mental model very different from the one they have in place. They'll need to rethink their notions of where value can be created and how they can capture that value (Hagel III, Armstrong, 1997).

The rapid growth of the Internet and associated technologies have created a new business environment and opened up myriad new possibilities for conducting and managing businesses. Terms such as digital economy, eBusiness, and eCommerce are being used to characterize these developments (WTO, 2001). Businesses have become internet worked eBusiness enterprises. The Internet and Internet-like networks inside the enterprise (intranets), between an enterprise and its trading partners (extranets), and other types of networks are now the primary information technology infrastructure of many organizations. The Internet is a network of networks. The internet worked eBusiness enterprise enables managers, business professionals, teams, and workgroups to electronically exchange data and information anywhere in the world with other end users, customers, suppliers, and business partners. Companies and workgroups can thus collaborate more creatively, manage their business operations and resources more effectively, and compete successfully in today's fast-changing global economy (O'Brien, 2001).

There are many benefits of bringing a business to the Internet. An eCommerce can offer personalization, high quality customer service and improved supply-chain management-the strategic management of distribution channels and processes that support them. Yahoo, EBay, Amazon.com, and other eCommerce sites have helped to define industry categories and business models on the Web (Deitel, Deitel, Steinbuhler, 2001).

Intellectual property plays an important role in an increasingly broad range of areas, ranging from the Internet to health care to nearly all aspects of science and technology and literature and the arts. Understanding the role of intellectual property in these areas–many of them still emerging–often requires significant new research and study. Copyright is a legal term describing rights given to creators for their literary and artistic works. The kinds of works covered by copyright include literary works such as novels, poems, plays, reference works, newspapers, and computer programs; databases; films, musical compositions, and choreography; artistic works such as paintings, drawings, photographs and sculpture; architecture; and advertisements, maps, and technical drawings (WIPO, 2001).

Copyright motivates the creative activity of authors and thereby provides the public with the products of those creators. By granting authors exclusive rights, the public receives the benefit of literature and music and other creative works that might not otherwise be created or disseminated. Effective copyright protection promotes a new Cyber-marketplace of ideas, expression, and products (IITF Report, 1995).

The Internet and other digital technologies raise new issues for copyright law because they permit new ways of creating, using, and duplicating works of authorship. Decentralized infringement—where copies can be made cheaply and distributed widely by individuals, as is possible on the Internet—presents the most significant challenge today for copyright law's accommodation of new technologies (Hardy, 1998). I. Trotter Hardy is a professor of law at the College of William and Mary School of Law. He specializes in intellectual property law as it relates to copyright, computers, and other technologies, and has written numerous articles on these issues. (Library of Congress, Washington, DC, http://www.loc.gov).

The information infrastructure has the potential to demolish careful balancing of public good and private interest that has emerged from the evolution of U.S. IP law over the past 200 years. Changes driven by rapid innovation amount to a leap that may well upset the current balance, forcing a rethinking of many fundamental premises and practices. If, as is often claimed, we are seeing an economic shift as significant as the industrial revolution, then intellectual property may well be the most important asset in the coming decades. Decisions we make now will determine who will benefit from the technology and who will have access to what information on what terms—foundational elements of our future society (NAP, 2000).

The Digital Millennium Copyright Act (DMCA) created a new feature in copyright law that has crystallized why so many academics, librarians, computer users, and technology entrepreneurs object to what they regard as the overreaching nature of copyright law (Clark, 2002).

The Internet has revolutionized the computer and communications world like nothing before. The invention of the telegraph, telephone, radio, and computer set the stage for this unprecedented integration of capabilities. The Internet is at once a world-wide broadcasting capability, a mechanism for information dissemination, and a medium for collaboration and interaction between individuals and their computers without regard for geographic location (ISOC, 2001).

The Internet is the result of visionary thinking by people in the early 1960s that saw great potential value in allowing computers to share information on research and development in scientific and military fields. J.C.R. Licklider of MIT, first proposed a global network of computers in 1962, and moved over to the Defense Advanced Research Projects Agency (DARPA) in late 1962 to head the work to develop it. The Internet, then known as ARPANET, was brought online in 1969 under a contract let by the renamed Advanced Research Projects Agency (ARPA) which initially connected four major computers at universities in the southwestern US: UCLA, Stanford Research Institute, UCSB, and the University of Utah (Howe, 2001).

E-mail was adapted for ARPANET by Ray Tomlinson in 1972. He picked the @ symbol from the available symbols on his Teletype to link the username and address. The Internet matured in the 70's as a result of the TCP/IP architecture first proposed by Bob Kahn at BBN and further developed by Kahn and Vint Cerf at Stanford and others throughout the 70's. It was adopted by the Defense Department in 1980 replacing the earlier Network Control Protocol (NCP) and universally adopted by 1983. Tim Berners-Lee and others at the European Laboratory for Particle Physics, more popularly known as CERN, proposed a new protocol for information distribution. This protocol, which became the World Wide Web in 1991, was based on hypertext-a system of embedding links in text to link to other text, which you have been using every time you selected a text link while reading these pages. The development in 1993 of the graphical browser Mosaic by Marc Andreessen and his team at the National Center For Supercomputing Applications (NCSA) gave the protocol its big boost. Later, Andreessen moved to become the brains behind Netscape Corp, which produced the most successful graphical type of browser and server until Microsoft declared war and developed its MicroSoft Internet Explorer (Howe, 2001).

Delphi was the first national commercial online service to offer Internet access to its subscribers. It opened up an email connection in July 1992 and full Internet service in November 1992. Commercialization of the Internet involved not only the development of competitive, private network services, but also the development of commercial products implementing the Internet technology. On October 24, 1995, the Federal Networking Council unanimously passed a resolution defining the term Internet. This definition was developed in consultation with members of the Internet and intellectual property rights communities. All pretenses of limitations on commercial use disappeared in May 1995 when the National Science Foundation ended its sponsorship of the Internet backbone, and all traffic relied on commercial networks. AOL, Prodigy, and CompuServe came online. Since commercial usage was so widespread by this time and educational institutions had been paying their own way for some time, the loss of NSF funding had no appreciable effect on costs (Howe, 2001).

The Internet represents one of the most successful examples of the benefits of sustained investment and commitment to research and development of information infrastructure. Beginning with the early research in packet switching, the government, industry and academia have been partners in evolving and deploying this exciting new technology. The Internet today is a widespread information infrastructure, the initial prototype of what is often called the National (or Global or Galactic) Information Infrastructure. Its history is complex and involves many aspects - technological, organizational, and community. And its influence reaches not only to the technical fields of computer communications but throughout society as we move toward increasing use of online tools to accomplish information acquisition, community operations and eCommerce. The most pressing question for the future of the Internet is not how the technology will change, but how the process of change and evolution itself will be managed. With the success of the Internet has come a proliferation of stakeholders-stakeholders now with an economic as well as an intellectual investment in the network (ISOC, 2002).

It is the arrival of the commercial use of the Internet, driven by its World Wide Web subset that has been defining new eCommerce since 1993. eCommerce) is sharing business information, maintaining business relationships, and conducting business transactions by means of telecommunications networks. Traditional eCommerce, conducted with the use of information technologies centering on electronic data interchange (EDI) over proprietary value-added networks, is rapidly moving to the Internet. The Internet's World Wide Web has become the prime driver of contemporary eCommerce, which has been vastly broadened and redefined by the use of the new medium (Zwass, 1996). eCommerce is a new and certainly trendy name, but the practice it refers to originated a half-century ago in the Berlin airlift (Seideman, 1996). This practice became electronic data interchange (EDI), the computer-to-computer exchange of standardized electronic transaction documents. Although what can now be called traditional eCommerce has not been limited to EDI and has included business practices built around computer-to-computer transmissions of variety of message forms, bar codes, and files, the use of EDI has arguably led to the most significant organizational transformations and market initiatives (Jelassi and Figon, 1994).

In a broader sense, all the major computer and telecommunications technologies, and database management in particular, under grid eCommerce. The set of technologies driving eCommerce is embodied today in the Internet. This conglomerate is a transformational technology that has challenged old assumptions and helps shape new workplaces, organizations, and markets. The Internet offers an open platform for new eCommerce, removing the long lead times, asset specificity, and bilateralism of eCommerce based on the traditional proprietary EDI (Fedorowicz and Konsynski, 1994). Global business-to-business eCommerce is expected to benefit hugely by moving forward from the simple transaction sets of the traditional EDI, which are basically electronic equivalents of paper forms, to far more elaborate, validated, and customizable business scenarios of open-EDI (Bons, Lee, Wagenaar, 1998).

Though only few years old, eCommerce has the potential to radically alter economic activities and social environments. Already it affects such large sectors as communications, finance, and retail trade. It holds promise in areas such as education, health and government. The greatest effects may be associated not with many of the impacts that command the most attention, e.g. customized products, the elimination of middleman, but with the less visible, and potentially more pervasive effects on routine business activities. The activities may include ordering office supplies, paying bills, and estimating demand, that is, on the way businesses interact. As technology improves, the current laws about intellectual property and copyright are being challenged. Copying of nearly everything, from sound, to text, to video is made simple with computers, the Internet, scanners, CD burners, and other technologies (WIPO, 2001).

The U.S. Department of Commerce estimated in the 1980s the worldwide value of pirated music to be $1.2 billion annually (Benko, 1987). The International Intellectual Property Alliance estimated U.S. losses in the recorded music industry due to piracy at $600 million per year in the 1980s and the numbers are certainly higher now (Benko, 1987). Laws regarding intellectual property are in place to protect expression of ideas as well as economic well being of companies, like record companies, who are dependent on intellectual property as a product to be sold. Estimations have reported "the theft of intellectual property rights in the United States cost over $300 billion dollars in 1997 alone" (Hsieh, 1998).

Technology has always presented a challenge to copyright laws, but the challenge has never been as difficult as now in the digital age. Music fans have always been able to circumvent copyright laws with analog taping of vinyl records and illegal pressing of records, but the change to digital formats complicate the issue. The change in format from vinyl records and tapes to compact discs (CDs) and digital audio technology (DAT) has impacted the quality of illegal copies of music. Also, the Internet, with its millions of users and ease of sharing files is a challenge to copyright legislation. Now, with the introduction of a new format (MP3 files), technology is allowing users to quickly and easily bypasses copyright laws regarding music (Samuelson, 1999).

Digital technology allows for clarity and quality not found in the old style of tape copying. While a tape eventually wear out and copies of copies gradually lose quality, digital copying eliminates these problems. While the first illegally copied CDs were copied from vinyl records (along with the crackles and pops of a record), digital noise reduction improved the quality of the recording. Instead of taping from records and losing quality because of surface noise, music copied and stored in digital-to-digital form does not reduce quality (Schwartz, 1999).

Five broad themes have emerged as important for understanding the eCommerce (OECD report, 1999):

1. eCommerce transforms the marketplace: eCommerce is changing the way business is conducted traditional intermediary functions will be replaced, new products and markets will be developed, and new and far closer relationships will be created between business and consumers. It will change the organization of work: new channels of knowledge diffusion and human interactivity in the workplace will be opened with more flexibility and adaptability will be needed, and workers' functions and skills will be redefined.

2. eCommerce has a catalytic effect. eCommerce will serve to accelerate and diffuse more widely changes that are already under way in the economy, such as the reform of regulations, the establishment of electronic links between businesses (EDI), the globalization of economic activity, and the demand for higher-skilled workers. Likewise, many sectoral trends already underway, such as e-banking, direct booking of travel, and one-to-one marketing, will be accelerated by eCommerce.

3. eCommerce over the Internet vastly increases interactivity in the economy. These linkages now extend down to small businesses and households and reach out to the world at large. Access will shift away from personal computers to cheap and easy-to-use TVs and telephones to devices yet to be invented. People will increasingly have the ability to communicate and transact business anywhere, anytime. This will have a profound impact, not the least of which will be the erosion of economic and geographic boundaries.

4. Openness is an underlying technical and philosophical tenet of the expansion of eCommerce. The widespread adoption of the Internet as a platform for business is due to its non-proprietary standards and open nature as well as to the huge industry that has evolved to support it. The economic power that stems from joining a large network will help to ensure that new standards remain open. More importantly, openness has emerged as a strategy, with many of the most successful eCommerce ventures granting business partner and consumers unparallel access to their inner workings, abases, and personnel. This has led to a shift in the role of consumers, who are increasingly implicated as partners in product design and creation. An expectation of openness is building on the part of consumers/citizens, which will cause transformations, for better (e.g. increased transparency, competition) or for worse (e.g. potential invasion of privacy) in the economy and society.

5. eCommerce alters the relative importance of time. Many of the routines that help define the look and feel of the economy and society are a function of time: mass production is the fastest way of producing at the lowest cost; one's community tends to be geographically determined because time is a determinant of proximity. eCommerce is reducing the importance of time by speeding up production cycles, allowing firms to operate in close coordination and enabling consumers to conduct transactions around the clock. As the role of time changes, so will the structure of business and social activities, causing potentially large impacts.

Intellectual Property Protection-Copyright

The Internet poses a threat to copyright laws, especially in the areas of illegal music copying and distribution. The Internet is made up of millions of sites with millions of users potentially viewing those sites daily. It is very easy for users to download information from other peoples' sites and in many cases this activity is not easily monitored. A user with a personal web page may also upload files to the server where the page is located and then allow other users to copy that file, regardless of the fact that it may be copyrighted (Samuelson, 1999).

During the 21st century, intellectual property will play an ever more important role on the international stage. Works of the mind-intellectual property-such as inventions, designs, trademarks, books, music, and films, are now used and enjoyed on every continent on earth. The World Intellectual Property Organization (WIPO), is an international organization dedicated to helping to ensure that the rights of creators and owners of intellectual property are protected worldwide and that inventors and authors are, thus, recognized and rewarded for their ingenuity. This international protection acts as a spur to human creativity, pushing forward the boundaries of science and technology and enriching the world of literature and the arts. By providing a stable environment for the marketing of intellectual property products, it also oils the wheels of international trade. The number of member States belonging to WIPO now stands at 179, over 90 percent of the world's countries-a reflection of the crucial importance and relevance attached to the work of the organization.

With a staff of some 817 drawn from around the world, WIPO carries out many tasks related to the protection of intellectual property rights, such as administering international treaties, assisting governments, organizations and the private sector, monitoring developments in the field and harmonizing and simplifying relevant rules and practices. In all that it does, the key words are relevance, efficiency, communication, and international cooperation. In the new millennium, WIPO faces many new challenges; one of the most urgent is the need for both the organization and its member states to adapt to and benefit from rapid and wide-ranging technological change, particularly in the field of information technology and the Internet. Under the leadership of its Director General, Dr. Kamil Idris, and with the close cooperation of its member states, WIPO is confident about meeting those challenges. In working towards its objectives, the organization will strive to contribute to the good of mankind by creating real wealth for nations, and to enhance the quality and enjoyment of life (WIPO, 2001).

Because the WIPO is the leading authority on this matter, the text of the convention establishing the WIPO definition of intellectual property states that intellectual property generally refers to rights relating to, among others, the following:

1. Literary, artistic, and scientific works

2. Performances by performing artists, phonograms, and broadcasts

3. Inventions in all fields of human endeavor

4. Scientific discoveries.

In other words, intellectual property, in the most general sense, encompasses creations of the human intellect (hence the term itself) and their protection, usually by copyright. The WIPO is responsible for both the protection of intellectual property internationally (by means of cooperation among its member nations) and the legal and administrative aspects of the protection. To this end, it administers various treaties, all which attempt to improve the protection of intellectual property.

Intellectual property, involves copyright. Copyright is a form of legal protection provided to the authors of *original* works, otherwise known as the owners of intellectual property. The international Berne Convention for the Protection of Literary and Artistic Works in 1971 established that works protected under copyright include:

1. Literary and artistic works, which includes every production in the literary, scientific, and artistic domain, whatever the mode of expression

2. Dramatic and dramatic-musical works

3. Choreographic works

4. Photographic works

5. Works of applied art.

The United States, a member state of WIPO, has established similar guidelines in its copyright law. Copyright is a form of protection provided by the laws of the United States (title 17, U.S. Code) to the authors of "original works of authorship," including literary, dramatic, musical, artistic, and certain other intellectual works. This protection is available to both published and unpublished works. Section 106 of the 1976 Copyright Act generally gives the owner of copyright the exclusive right to do and to authorize others to do the following:

- To reproduce the work in copies or phonorecords;

- To prepare derivative works based upon the work;

- To distribute copies or phonorecords of the work to the public by sale or other transfer of ownership, or by rental, lease, or lending;

- To perform the work publicly, in the case of literary, musical, dramatic, and choreographic works, pantomimes, and motion pictures and other audiovisual works;

- To display the copyrighted work publicly, in the case of literary, musical, dramatic, and choreographic works, pantomimes, and pictorial, graphic, or sculptural works, including the individual images of a motion picture or other audiovisual work; and

- In the case of sound recordings, to perform the work publicly by means of a digital audio transmission.

In addition, certain authors of works of visual art have the rights of attribution and integrity as described in section 106A of the 1976 Copyright Act. For further information, request Circular 40, "Copyright Registration for Works of the Visual Arts."

It is illegal for anyone to violate any of the rights provided by the copyright law to the owner of copyright. These rights, however, are not unlimited in scope. Sections 107 through 121 of the 1976 Copyright Act establish limitations on these rights. In some cases, these limitations are specified exemptions from copyright liability. One major limitation is the doctrine of fair use, which is given a statutory basis in section 107 of the 1976 Copyright Act. In other instances, the limitation takes the form of a "compulsory license" under which certain limited uses of copyrighted works are permitted upon payment of specified royalties and compliance with statutory conditions. For further information about the limitations of any of these rights, consult the copyright law or write to the Copyright Office (U.S. Copyright Office–Copyright Basics).

The U.S. Constitution gives Congress the power to grant authors a broad term designating creators of works certain rights regarding their works in order to "promote the progress of science and the useful arts" (Article 1, Section 8). Copyrights are used to protect the "expression of ideas," not specifically ideas themselves (Benko, 1987). Title 17 of the United States Code (U.S.C.) deals specifically with copyrights. The laws surrounding copyright are discussed more extensively in Chapter 2.

The three basic requirements for a work to be copyrighted including fixation, originality, and expression. A work is "fixed" if it is "sufficiently permanent or stable to permit it to be perceived, reproduced, or otherwise communicated for a period of more than transitory duration" (17 U.S.C. ß 101-Appendix B). Basically, a work must be in a form that could be copied in order to receive protection from unauthorized copying. It is also useful to note that the U.S.C. maintains that a work is protected by copyright if it is fixed by any method now known or later developed or even if the work can be perceived only "with the aid of a machine or device," such as a compact disc played on a player (17 U.S.C. ß 101). Originality indicates that a work must owe origins to the person claiming to be the author. It does not imply that "a work must be new, startling, novel, or unusual". It just must not be a copy of someone else's work. The idea of expression, to be copyrighted, must be a specific expression of an idea, not just an idea. The conditions of idea expression are found in 17 U.S.C. ß 102 (b). These conditions are: in no case does copyright protection for an original work of authorship extend to any idea, procedure, process, system, method of operation, concept, principle, or discovery, regardless of the form in which it is described, explained, illustrated, or embodied in such work (U.S. Copyright Office).

This study presents the digital copyright issues that must successfully be addressed in order for eCommerce to flourish. It provides researchers and policy makers with a qualitative picture of the current state and likely future direction of eCommerce and its impact on intellectual property (IP) copyright. On this basis, researchers and policy makers can begin to outline the parameters of its impact and identify areas in need of future research. This chapter addresses how these areas intertwine and connect.

<u>The Entertainment Industry</u>

A definition of "the entertainment industry" is provided since the industry is divided up into three different categories. The three divisions include the artists, the record companies, and music fans. Artists are the individuals who initially create the work (e.g. music and lyrics); these artists can include bands, individuals, musicians, and songwriters. The record companies are organizations that "sign" artists to work for them. The artist signs a contract where generally the record companies agree to promote and distribute works if the artist agrees to give up the copyrights of their music to the company. If the record company promotes the work effectively it will sell well in the stores. In return for the promotion a percentage of the money from each purchase accrues to the record company and another percentage to the artist. The costs of the making of the work are also covered by the consumer price. The consumer, the third part of "the entertainment industry," supports both the record companies and the artists when purchasing CDs, tapes, and other related merchandise (Lucy and Maher, 1997).

Among the content industries affected by the digital environment, the music industry has, for a variety of reasons been thrown first into the maelstrom. Events have proceeded at the dizzying pace that has been called "Internet time," with technical, legal, social, and industrial developments occurring in rapid-fire succession. Yet the problems facing the music industry will likely soon be found on the doorstep of other content industries. This chapter presents the developments in the music industry and reviews its early phases of coming to grips with digital information. These developments offer intriguing information illustrating the problems, opportunities, possible solutions, and the cast of characters involved in dealing with digital intellectual property (IP). The focus is not on the day-to-day specifics, as these sometimes change more rapidly than daily newspapers can track. Instead, the perspective is on the underlying phenomena, as a way of understanding the issues more generally. Not all of these issues will play out identically in different industries. But some of the problems will be widespread because they are intrinsic to digital information, no matter what content it carries. The problems include distributing digital information without losing control of it, struggles over standards and formats, and evolving the shape of industries as the new technology changes the previous balance of power (Lucy and Maher, 1997).

The innovations that have made the Internet possible have not only brought fundamental changes to communications, but have also fueled dramatic developments for the new digital economy. These developments are reflected in financial markets and trade flows, innovative models for business, as well as in new opportunities for consumers. The remarkable scope of these developments has made eCommerce a subject of significant economic, policy, and social importance. Commerce conducted across electronic media is not new. However, the advent of the Internet, a "network of networks" using open standards, has given rise to a prodigious international expansion in the number of users and range of applications relevant to daily life. In many regions of the globe, it has begun to change significantly the ways in which individuals, companies and governments organize their affairs, interact, and conduct business (WIPO, 2001).

According to industry researcher Gartner, the one billionth PC was shipped in April 2002, while flat growth of late is expected to pick up pace, as broadband penetration increases and emerging markets adopt PCs at feverish rates. While it took 25 years for one billion PCs to ship, Gartner predicts the two billionth PC will ship in just six years' time.

Gartner banks on the industry overcoming some tough recent times by looking to countries like China (Gartner-Dataquest, June 28, 2002).

Buyers spent $2.7 billion to acquire 121 Internet-related properties in April 2002 as mergers and acquisitions activity spurted to its highest level in the last six months. The spurts of mergers and acquisitions activity in the online destinations sector are part of a real revival in faith in certain dot-com business models that were scorned during the summer 2000 Internet shakeout. The pattern seems to be growing in online travel, e-recruiting and in e-finance. Activity remained strong in Internet infrastructure including e-business enablement tools and applications and wireless Internet properties (Webmergers.com, June 30, 2002).

The estimated number of transactions completed on the Internet in 2001 is approximately $8 billion. The estimated number of people online in the United States in 2000 was 63.2 million. In 2001, there were 498 million people online worldwide–34 percent are in the U.S. (169 million U.S. online users). The estimated dollar value of transactions on the Internet predicted for 2005 is $155.6 billion. The number of households with expected DSL Service in 2005 will be 36 million subscribers with estimated 21 billion in revenues (CyberAtlas, May 20, 2002).

Research forecasts predict that the volume of eCommerce transactions will differ dramatically (Electronic Transactions, 2002). However, the business-to-consumer sector is dwarfed by the extraordinary revenue predictions for business-to-business eCommerce, B2B-EC, (Bontis and Castro, 2000). The Boston Consulting Group estimates that B2B eCommerce will reach $2.8 trillion by 2003, with a huge increase in transactions conducted over the Internet rather than via EDI (King, 1999). By 2004, B2B-EC will constitute 7 percent of the world's total sales revenue (Bontis and Castro, 2000). Forrester Research predicts that revenue from B2B transactions on the Internet will be over $1,551 billion by 2003, whereas

B2C eCommerce will bring in only 7.4 percent as much (Warkentin et al, 2001). Gartner Group reports that in 1999, worldwide B2B-EC reached $145 billion, with the North America region accounting for 63 percent of the market. However, Gartner Group also reports that in 2004, worldwide B2B-EC is projected to surpass $7.29 trillion, with the North America region accounting for just 39 percent of that market (Fridman, 2000).

The Gartner Group projects that, by the end of 2002, nearly 26 percent of all US companies will use the Internet to deliver B2B invoices (Bonisteel, 2001). According to IDC's report, Asia Pacific excluding Japan, B2B transactions will be over $516 billion of direct and indirect materials through the Internet by 2005 which represents greater than a 39 times increase over the $12.8 billion spent in 2000 (Edwards, 2001). According to this analysis, transactions through B2B-EC in the coming years will grow rapidly and will become a significant media to carry out electronic transactions (Electronic Transactions, 2002).

Pre-Problem Statement

The ease of modifying or copying digitized material and the proliferation of computer networking has raised fundamental questions about copyright-intellectual property protections rooted in the U.S. Constitution. The Internet also poses serious economic issues for those who create and market that material (NAP, 2000). Two events motivate reexamining the concepts, policies, and practices associated with intellectual property impacted by eCommerce:

a. Advances in technology have produced radical shifts in the ability to reproduce, distribute, control, and publish information. Information in digital form has radically changed the economics and ease of reproduction. Reproduction costs are much lower for both rights holders (content owners) and infringers alike. Computer networks have radically changed the economics of distribution. With transmission speeds approaching a billion characters per second, networks enable sending information products worldwide, cheaply and almost instantaneously. The World Wide Web has radically changed the economics of publication, allowing everyone to be a publisher with worldwide reach.

b. With its commercialization and integration into everyday life, the information infrastructure has run headlong into intellectual property law. Today, some actions that can be taken casually by the average citizen-downloading files, forwarding information found on the Web-can at times be blatant violations of intellectual property laws; others, such as making copies of information for private use, may require subtle and difficult interpretation of the law simply to determine their legality. Individuals in their daily lives have the capability and the opportunity to access and copy vast amounts of digital information, yet lack a clear picture of what is acceptable or legal. Nor is it easy to supply a clear answer because (among other things) current intellectual property law is complex.

II. Statement of the Problem:

In a fundamental respect, the international character of eCommerce raises questions about the nature of traditional legal systems in general, and intellectual property law in particular. Both are based on notions of sovereignty and territoriality. The Internet, in contrast, like the movement of weather within the global climate, largely ignores distinctions based on territorial borders. Instead, infrastructure, code and language have thus far had a greater bearing on the reach of its currents (WIPO, 2001). For example, the most fundamental issue raised for the fields of copyright is the determination of the scope of protection in the digital environment involving how rights are defined, and what exceptions and limitations are permitted. Other important issues include how rights are enforced and administered in this environment; who in the chain of dissemination of infringing material can be held legally responsible for the infringement; and questions of jurisdiction and applicable law.

The protection of copyright and related rights covers a wide array of human creativity. Much of the creative content that fuels eCommerce is subject to such protection. Under the most important international copyright convention, the Berne Convention copyright protection covers all literary and artistic works. This term encompasses diverse forms of creativity, such as writings, both fiction and non-fiction, including scientific and technical texts and computer programs; databases that are original due to the selection or arrangement of their contents; musical works; audiovisual works; works of fine art, including drawings and paintings; and photographs. Related rights protect the contributions of others who add value in the presentation of literary and artistic works to the public including performing artists, such as actors, dancers, singers and musicians; the producers of phonograms, including CDs; and broadcasting organizations also affected by copyright laws and regulations.

Digital technology enables the transmission and use of protected materials in digital form over interactive networks. While the transmission of text, sound, images, and computer programs over the Internet is already commonplace, this will soon also be true for transmission of multimedia works such as feature films, as the technical constraints of narrow bandwidth begin to disappear. Materials protected by copyright and related rights, spanning the range of information and entertainment products, will constitute much of the valuable subject matter of eCommerce.

A. Research Question

What is the impact of eCommerce on intellectual property?

B. Sub-Problems

The development of digital technologies, permitting transmission of works over networks (by definition, when a work is transmitted from one point to another, or made available for the public to access, numerous parties are involved in the transmission) has raised questions about how these rights apply in the new environment. eCommerce generates interactivity and transactions between parties who may have had no previous contact. Even small businesses may now be considered as multi-national enterprises, in a zero gravity digital environment in which business can enter into agreements with parties located all over the world. These dealings can occur in real-time over the network between businesses, or between businesses and consumers. Many of these transactions may be nothing more than one-off agreements, in which there is no immediate contemplation by either party that a continuing relationship will result from the transaction.

These Internet transactions need rules to govern the relationships between the parties regarding the copyright. The primary vessel for these rules is the agreement itself – the contract. There is an increasing recognition of the pivotal role that contracts can play in the international market of eCommerce (WIPO, 2001). As a means of giving expression to the principle of party autonomy, and allowing for decentralized decision-making in relation to commercial rights and obligations, the contract provides a flexible yet legally enforceable mechanism. In this respect, contracts may be viewed as the most important self-regulatory measure available to parties engaging in eCommerce.

Many contracts in eCommerce implicate the intellectual property rights of one or more of the parties to the contract. A contract for the use of intellectual property rights may assume various forms. Licenses, assignments, distribution, and franchising agreements, and joint venture arrangements are some of the most common forms. For example, a license is a contract authorizing the licensee to do something that, in the absence of the license, would normally constitute an infringement of the licensor's intellectual property right. When consumers on the Internet access a musical composition, they may do so pursuant to a license agreement.

The business distributing the music, in turn, may hold licenses from the copyright owner and the producer of the sound recording. Given the many countries in which participating businesses and consumers may reside, and the numerous national and local laws concerning both the law of contracts and intellectual property, contracting in the digital medium has the potential to be a more complicated endeavor than contracting in the offline world (WIPO, 2001).

The rights that apply in the new environment include entities that provide Internet access or online services. In particular, when multiple copies are made as works traverse the networks:

Q1. Does each and every copy implicate the reproduction right?

Q2. Is there communication to the public when a work (art, music) is not broadcast, but simply made available to individual members of the public if and when they wish to see or hear it?

Q3. Is it a public performance when different individuals on the monitors of their personal computers or other digital devices view a work at different times?

Q4. Are existing exceptions and limitations, written in language conceived for other circumstances?

Q5. When service providers participate in transmitting or making available materials provided by another, which infringes upon copyright or related rights, are they liable for the infringement?

C. Hypothesis

Given the capabilities and characteristics of digital network technologies, eCommerce will have a tremendous impact on the system of copyright and related rights, and the scope of copyright in turn may have an effect on how eCommerce will evolve. If legal rules are not set and applied appropriately, digital technology has the potential to undermine the basic tenets of copyright. The Internet has been described as the world's biggest copy machine. The older technologies of photocopying and taping allow mechanical copying by individual consumers, but in limited quantities, requiring considerable time, and of a lower quality than the original. Moreover, the copies were physically located in the same place as the person making the copy. On the Internet, in contrast, one can make an unlimited number of copies, virtually instantaneously, without perceptible degradation in quality. And these copies can be transmitted to locations around the world in a matter of minutes. The result could be the disruption of traditional markets for the sale of copies of programs, software, music, art, books, and movies.

It is therefore critical to not only research this specific IP issue but also recommend adjustment in the U.S. legal system to respond to the new technological environment in an effective and appropriate way, because technologies and markets evolve rapidly. This will ensure the continued furtherance of the fundamental guiding principles of copyright, which remain constant whatever the technology of the day: a. providing incentives to creators to produce and disseminate new creative materials; b. recognizing the importance of their contributions, by giving them reasonable control over the exploitation of those materials and allowing them to profit from them; c. providing appropriate balance for the public interest, particularly education, research, and access to information; d. and thereby ultimately benefiting society by promoting the development of culture, science, and the economy.

Accordingly, the goal proposed for policy makers would be to achieve an appropriate balance in the law, providing strong and effective rights, but within reasonable limits and with fair exceptions.

Trade in copyrighted works, performances and phonograms will become a major element of global eCommerce, which will grow and thrive along with the value of the material that is traded. If rights holders are secure in their ability to sell and license their property over the Internet, they will exploit this market fully and make more and more valuable works available through this medium. Appropriate limitations and exceptions will continue to safeguard public interest uses. The result will be a benefit to consumers, a benefit to rights holders, a benefit to service providers, and a benefit to national economies.

D. Research Methodology Statement

The qualitative research methodology designed for the study was based on content analysis procedures. These procedures provide methods of data collection, organization and analysis process to identify and better understand the current complex intellectual property copyright laws and regulations, as described in the statement of the problem on Page 26. The technique of content analysis includes the domain of textual analysis (Wheelock, Haney, & Bebell, 2000). Content analysis enables researchers to sift through large volumes of data with relative ease in a systematic fashion (GAO, 1996). It can be a useful technique that designed to discover and describe the focus of individuals, groups, institutions, or social attention (Weber, 1990). Content analysis has been defined as a systematic technique for compressing many words of text into fewer content categories (Berelson, 1952; Krippendorff, 1980; and Weber, 1990). Holsti (1969) offers a broad definition of content analysis as, "any technique for making inferences by objectively and systematically identifying specified characteristics of messages" (p. 14).

The focus and nature of the research process was context based. The method of data collection included information from published literature, sample surveys, intellectual property copyright court cases, articles, and Internet specific publications, the Internet itself, newspapers and trade journals. The study made specific observations with regard to intellectual property and then drew inferences about larger and more general copyright laws and regulations, and eBusiness models phenomena specifically. The findings, conclusions and recommendations are descriptive and communicated by interpretative narratives from the data and individual quotes, as needed to address the research question.

A fuller description of the methodology employed is addressed in Chapter 3.

III. Purpose of the Study

The purpose of this study is to examine the impact of eCommerce on intellectual property Copyright laws and regulations. The copyright laws and regulations enter in a new era of management and enforcement, where technology could be envisioned to provide an answer to safeguard the intellectual property rights threatened by the same technology. This study researched digital commerce impact and its consequences on the legal regime of copyright laws.

Intellectual property is a property that is protected under federal law, including copyrightable works, ideas, discoveries, and inventions. Vigilant monitoring of developments is needed to assess whether action is necessary or appropriate to preserve and enhance the effectiveness of intellectual property in this new digital environment.

Intellectual property both affects and is affected by eCommerce in a multiplicity of ways. Defining the proper scope of intellectual property copyrights in relation to the new and rapidly evolving digital technologies and content, and devising means for the protection of those rights that are appropriate in light of the international dimensions of eCommerce, is a venture that will engage the intellectual property copyrights issue for years to come.

IV. Scope and Limitations of the Study

This report is limited to the study of Intellectual Property Copyright laws and regulations. There is a healthy debate going on in an attempt to realize the promise of the information age. This study seeks to explain and explore the range of technological and business tools that may be useful and recommend a variety of actions that can be taken to help ensure that the benefits of the information infrastructure are realized for rights holders and society as a whole. The focus on copyright derives from the observation that copyright protects a large variety of the intellectual property frequently encountered by the public and has the highest visibility in the debates over intellectual property and the information infrastructure. One of the consequences of global networks is the inevitable interaction between U.S. law and culture and those of other countries. This can be problematic because laws and intellectual property practice differ widely across countries and are likely to remain different despite efforts at harmonization (NAP, 2000).

This study builds on previous studies in the area of intellectual property and information technology. The most recent effort was undertaken by the Information

Infrastructure Task Force, which issued the report "Intellectual Property and the National Information Infrastructure" (IITF, 1995). The IITF white paper presents the detailed legal issues concerning copyright and digital technology, but it does not address business models, protection technologies, or other issues in any particular depth. In addition, the U.S. Copyright Office commissioned a study on the future of copyright in the networked world (Hardy, 1998). That report, which provides good descriptive coverage of the relevant technologies and trends and some discussion on the pertinent economic and legal issues, identified trends but did not provide conclusions and recommendations.

Furthermore, a National Research Council (NRC) published a report-The Digital Dilemma: Intellectual Property in the Information Age. The report written by a study committee was commissioned to consider intellectual property rights broadly in the context of the emerging information infrastructure (NAP, 2000). The report did not provide Copyright solutions to controversial Digital Millinium Copyright (DMCA) Act of 1998. More recently, National Journal's Technology Daily published an article: 'How Copyright became controversial' (Clark, 2002). That report, which provides good descriptive coverage of the DMCA and current copyright court cases but did not provide specific copyright conclusions and recommendations from an eCommerce perspective.

This study does not duplicate the detailed legal analyses of the IITF white paper or the extensive review of technologies in the Hardy report or the detailed review of online business models in the NAP report or the detailed review of DMCA in the Clark report. Instead, it analyzes the work of IITF, Hardy, NAP and Clark reports regarding the IP copyright framework and offers a specific evaluation and construction of eBusiness models, public policy, technological protection measures, conclusions and recommendations designed to help all copyright stakeholders.

The PDE is organized into the following sections:

a. Chapter 2 provides a descriptive review of the literature and groundwork regarding the eCommerce and intellectual property issues.

b. Chapter 3 presents the methodology and data collection to accomplish this study.

c. Chapter 4 describes the analysis and results used to arrive at the prescribed outcomes.

d. Chapter 5 details the interpretation, conclusions, and recommendations for future research and Project Demonstrating Excellence summary.

e. Appendix A presents the references.

V. Chapter Summary:

The role of information products and services in the US economy is vast and still growing rapidly. The addition of an information sector category to the federal government's new industry classification system recognizes both the sector's economic importance and the fundamental kinship of publishing (print and software), motion picture and sound recording, radio and television broadcasting, libraries, and information and data processing services. The widespread use of computer networks and the global reach of the World Wide Web have added substantially to the information sector's production of an astonishing abundance of information in digital form, as well as offering unprecedented ease of access to it. Creating, publishing, distributing, using, and reusing information have become many times easier and faster in the past decade. The good news is the enrichment that this explosive growth in information brings to society as a whole. The bad news is the enrichment that it can also bring to those who take advantage of the properties of digital information and the Web to copy, distribute, and use information illegally. The Web is an information resource of extraordinary size and depth, yet it is also an information reproduction and dissemination facility of great reach and capability; it is at once one of the world's largest libraries and surely the world's largest copying machine.

This study adopts a broad-based understanding of electronic means to conduct eCommerce, focusing in particular on the expanding and international commercial activities taking place over open networks. From the intellectual property perspective, this focus on open networks generates great potential for new commercial opportunities; which may also pose significant risks for infringement of protected rights.

The issues described in this report are difficult and contentious because the stakes are high and the needs and desires of various stakeholders often are in conflict. The traditional tool for dealing with use and misuse of information is intellectual property copyright law, the constellation of statutes, and case law that govern copyrights. Part of the case for granting rights in intellectual property is the belief that protecting IP promotes the development of new products and services, and that erosion of those rights could threaten the economic performance of the business and curtail the major benefits it has brought. But as this study argues, with this new abundance of information and the ease with which it can be accessed, reproduced, and distributed have come problems that must be seen in all of their complexity, including related economic, social, technical, and philosophical concerns, as well as the accompanying legal and policy challenges.

Although debates over these issues are important, the focus of the study is limited to IP copyright laws and regulations because the IP copyright outcome will have a significant impact on developing eCommerce sector companies and help determine the character of the digital economy of the future as substantiated in the next chapter, Literature Review.

Chapter 2: Descriptive Literature Review

I. Introduction

The primary objective of the literature review is to understand the current state of intellectual property copyright issues impacted by commercial electronic transactions and their long-range implications for business. In addition, issues of validity by relating the study outcomes to previous research efforts are addressed.

II. Literature Review

That portion of the Internet known as the World Wide Web has been riding an exponential growth curve since 1994 (Network Wizards, 1999; Rutkowski, 1998), coinciding with the introduction of NCSA's graphically based software interface Mosaic for "browsing" the World Wide Web (Hoffman, 1995). As electronic commerce takes off, there is a tilt away from just offering advice and toward completing the sale online. While influence on purchases is still the biggest online impact, making the sale is the fastest growing category (Hanson, 2000).

eCommerce is commerce, but it is commerce accelerated and enhanced by information technology (IT), in particular the Internet. It enables customers, consumers, and companies to form powerful new relationships that would not be possible without the enabling technologies. Fundamentally, it is all still about commerce, people buying and selling products and services from and to each other. The Internet facilitates commerce by its great ability to move digital information at low cost (Haag, Cummmings, McCubbrey, 2002).

eCommerce is simply any business transaction that takes place via digital processes over a network and is not merely exchanging products or services for funds over the Internet.

According to Trepper (2000), eCommerce is "an enabling technology that allows businesses to increase the accuracy and efficiency of business transaction processing". eCommerce is also a way for organizations to exchange information with customers and suppliers to the benefit of everyone involved.

The emergence of Internet has removed geographical and physical boundaries to some extent by enabling people from different countries to communicate with each other electronically and to retrieve information quickly and easily (Gattiker, 2000). The rapid development and wide adoption of the Internet technology have brought new business opportunities. The trend of market globalization and the increasing emphasis of knowledge management have quickened the business and economic process worldwide (Bhatt, 2001).

The Internet-based system are computer applications that use the Internet technology, its universal connectivity, and the capabilities of the Web browser to integrate business processes within and beyond an enterprise for the sole purpose of business transactions and integration between the enterprise and its business partners (Fraser et al., 2000). In a turbulent, highly competitive and global market, manufacturers are facing the pressure from stakeholders asking them to "reduce and control" their costs, yet at the same time improve customer service, shorten product development cycle time, and enhance product quality (Griffiths et al., 2001; Bhatt, 2001).

The ability of a manufacturer to satisfy customer requirements in terms of order quantity, delivery lead-time, product design, and product quality, are essential to stay in business (Koh et al., 2000). The changing environment of the business market with its focus on costs, quality, flexibility and technology to meet the competitive challenges is causing major changes in inter-organizational business relationships. Many manufacturers are developing closer relationships with their suppliers and customers with the application of business-to-business and business to consumer systems and other inter-organizational information systems (IOS) (Han, 1997; Bhatt, 2001).

In the business-to-business eCommerce environment, IOS have been used since the early 1970s to link one or more manufacturers to their customers or suppliers through leased lines, mainframes, and legacy application code (Walton and Gapta, 1999; Loebbecke and Schäfer, 2001). IOS makes use of standard protocols to exchange information among the enterprise and its business partners through computer-to-computer exchange of electronic documents such as sales orders, purchase orders, shipping invoices, stock availability, financial information, and other data (Halhead, 1995; Bhatt and Emdad, 2001). The range of application of IOS has now extended from simply handling transaction data to supporting all forms of information exchange, including procurement transactions, supply chain management, sourcing information, new product development, and shared electronic mail (Archer and Yuan, 2000).

Rapid development of IOS in the form of Internet-base is driving much of business-to-business eCommerce (b2b-ec) and business-to-consumer eCommerce (b2c-ec) in the new millennium. Fiedler et al., (1999) show that "an important aspect in b2b-ec scenarios is how to meet response time and throughput requirements of applications in spite of execution taking place across corporate boundaries and, in the future, via the Internet instead of using leased lines". They believe that b2b-ec is transforming from traditional electronic data interchange (EDI)-based practice to a more challenging Internet-based approach. This approach is based on the notion of enterprise networks, where different companies pool their services to offer complex, value-added products.

The innovative development of Internet is to connect more than 100 million computers across the world to facilitate quick and inexpensive access to information and to enable the exchange of information (Fraser et al., 2000). eCommerce does not only lower the cost of trading significantly but more importantly it allows restructuring of the supply chain, business processes, and the nature of the business. Its effective deployment requires an understanding of the way in which the company operates now and a vision of the way it will be able to operate in the future (Fisher, 2000).

eCommerce generally refers to an inter-organizational information system that is intended to facilitate business-to-business and business-to-consumer electronic communication, information exchange and transaction support through a web of either public access or private value-added networks (Min and Galle, 1999). Many technologies can be used to support eCommerce. As described by the Electronic Commerce Association, it may involve streamlining processes, interconnectivity, Internet, EDI, electronic funds transfer, (EFT), e-mail, security, electronic document management, (EDM), workflow processing, middleware, bar-coding, imaging processing, smart cards, voice responses, and networking (Hsieh and Lin, 1998). B2b-ec includes a broad range of inter-organization transactions, including wholesale trade as well as company purchases of services, resources, technology, manufactured parts and components, and capital equipment (Lucking-Riley and Spulber, 2000).

For successful b2b or b2c-ec transactions, information must be exchanged and interpreted both within and between organizational and consumer boundaries (Drummond, 2000). Traditionally organizations have used paper forms to exchange information which created problems of slow transaction and extensive human handling, hence they have realized the importance of finding a more effective way to communicate and process transaction data

(Kappelman et al., 1996). EDI is "a form of electronic communication that allows businesses to exchange transaction data and documents in structured formats that can be processed by computer applications software" (Lankford and Johnson, 2000).

Recent development of the Internet and World Wide Web (WWW) has made eCommerce application over the Internet much more popular and low cost (Bhatt and Emdad, 2001). For smaller suppliers, electronic commerce technology can be helpful in allowing them to club together with other small manufacturers to provide an excellent platform so as to collaborate and work together to solve the problems they all face in exchange of information with their major business partners (Loughlin, 1999). Some manufacturers have considerable experience with some of the original b2b-ec technologies, such as EDI, but are finding the adoption of Internet-based forms of eCommerce a more complex process than they had anticipated (Chan and Swatman, 2000).

In the traditional eCommerce model, it was too expensive for many firms to be connected to a value added network in order to communicate with customers or suppliers. That barrier was crossed by the widespread interconnectivity and accessibility of the Internet. Within minutes, even small firms with a personal computer and Web browser can access a Web site, fill out purchase order forms, verify their credentials, complete secure transactions, and receive confirmation from trading partners. The Internet, a network of networks, has excellent "throughput capabilities" such as e-mail, file transfer, World Wide Web, and remote log-ins. The factors in favor of EDI/eCommerce include requiring lower cost, the availability of many more trading partners as it enables immediate connections between a wider range of participants, and a single network infrastructure to do both regular e-mail messaging and EDI (Ratnasingham, 1998; Angeles, 2000).

Laws regarding intellectual property are in place to protect expression of ideas as well as economic well being of companies, like record companies, which are dependent on intellectual property as a product to be sold. Estimations have reported "the theft of intellectual property rights in the United States cost over $300 billion dollars in 1997 alone" (Hsieh, 2001).

Intellectual property law cannot be patched, retrofitted, or expanded to contain digitized expression any more than real estate law might be revised to cover the allocation of broadcasting spectrum. We will need to develop an entirely new set of methods as befits this entirely new set of circumstances (Barlow, 1996). There are deep contradictions between the definition of an 'intellectual property right,' that is, a state-backed monopoly handed out to individuals or firms, and the popular neo-liberal vision that valorizes 'privatization' and free market economics (Aoki, 1998). The foundations of the economic case for intellectual property rights are questionable (Leith, 1997).

The global period of intellectual property is marked by a weakening, at least in relation to property, of the principles of territoriality and sovereignty. Intellectual property owners are finding that the intellectual property systems around the world are beginning to converge on the same substantive standards (Drano's, 1997). Digital media have unleashed deep-running changes in the international regime of intellectual property. The patchwork of nation states can no longer respond, with its purely territorial laws, to network imperatives of interconnectivity (Geller, 1998).

The economic pressures and the growing international significance of copyright have led to new laws. These new laws are overwhelmingly in furtherance of expanding protection, easier protection, and longer protection (Crews, 1998). Globalization of intellectual property laws is leading to an erosion of state sovereignty or, at least, "profound transformations" in our notions of sovereignty (Aoki, 1998a; Aoki, 1998b). Digital information not only ignores national borders, but also those of states, territories, and even individual institutions. Governments are finding it increasingly difficult, and in some cases impossible, to regulate information effectively at the very time that the economic power of information is increasing the political pressure for them to do so. The globalization of information may be rendering the traditional concept of the sovereignty of the nation-state obsolete (Cate, 1998).

To understand all of the issues relating to intellectual property and technology, one must first be familiar with the current laws regarding copyright. The World Intellectual Property Organization (WIPO) has international standards for intellectual property and has most jurisdictions over international agreements, but there is no official body to enforce intellectual property laws (Hseih, 2001). The WIPO encourages member nations, including the U.S., to make and update their domestic laws to protect intellectual property and also encourages cooperation between member nations by centralizing the administration of such laws. There are currently 171 members. No specific set of international laws regulates worldwide copyright protection, which is dependent on the law of individual nation; however, there are generally accepted agreements between nations. The Berne Convention was an original agreement regarding intellectual property. In effect since 1886, the Berne Convention administered by the WIPO. The Berne covers protection of literary and artistic works very broadly and establishes three main principles: national treatment, no conditional protection, and protection independent of the existence of protection in the country of origin.

There have been various other international treaties and conventions regarding copyright and intellectual property laws that the U.S. has signed and which specifically concern music and copyright. The Geneva Convention, Convention for the Protection of Producers of Phonograms Against Unauthorized Duplication of Their Phonogram, and the WIPO Performances and Phonograms Treaty all deal with intellectual property. The WIPO treaties have been adopted as law in the form of the Digital Millennium Copyright Act in the United States, adopted in 1998. Title 17 of the Unites States Code (U.S.C.) contains the copyright laws of the United States in substantial detail. This section of the law explains how copyright laws apply in the United States. There are many sections and clauses in Title 17 and those relevant to the research topic are discussed.

When an author creates a work he or she is granted exclusive rights and entitlements. Copyright holders are entitled to the following rights under the law (17 U.S.C. ß 106):

- to reproduce the copyrighted work in copies or phonorecords;
- to prepare derivative works based upon the copyrighted work;
- to distribute copies or phonorecords of the copyrighted work to the public by sale or other transfer of ownership, or by rental, lease, or lending;
- in the case of literary, musical, dramatic, and choreographic works, pantomimes, and motion pictures and other audiovisual works, to perform the copyrighted work publicly;
- in the case of literary, musical, dramatic, and choreographic works, pantomimes, and pictorial, graphic, or sculptural works, including the individual images of a motion picture or other audiovisual work, to display the copyrighted work publicly; and
- in the case of sound recordings, to perform the copyrighted work publicly by means of a digital audio transmission.

In areas such as book publishing and music, the author usually signs over his or her rights to the work, giving the publisher or record company the ownership of the copyright. This entitles the company to all of the rights of a copyright holder. There are some rights for users of copyrighted material, but they are limited to exceptions made for "fair use." Title 17 Section 107 defines fair use based on four main criteria and three tests. The four criteria are the purpose and character of the use, the nature of the copyrighted work, the amount and substantiality of the material used, and the effect of the use on the potential market of the work. The three tests used for judging fair use are brevity (amount copied), spontaneity (was there enough time to have asked for permission), and cumulative effect (the overall effect on the potential market of an author from unauthorized copying). These exceptions provide exceptions for educational purposes, libraries, and some other non-profit uses.

There is also the "first sale doctrine" which gives the original user (purchaser) the distribution rights to the copyrighted work (such as a CD). Section 109 of the U.S. Code gives the specifics of the law. Some important factors are that only the distribution right is given to the owner, not to any others such as the performers. For example, if a person purchases a video, the first sale doctrine does not cover the public showing of that video. Also, if the owner rents copyrighted material to a friend, that friend does not have the first sale rights of distribution, so they cannot copy and sell it.

The United States updated its laws with the passage of the Digital Millennium Copyright Act (DMCA) on October 28, 1998. The DMCA strengthened some weaknesses in Title 17 of the U.S. Code regarding effects of new technology on intellectual property and copyright. The DMCA established new regulations to deal with technology and copyright laws, much to the satisfaction of those with interests in the music industry and copyright defenders (Garnet, Holland, Bergman, 1997).

The DCMA (which is officially titled as "A bill to amend Title 17, U.S. Code, to implement the World Intellectual Property Organization Copyright Treaty and Performances and Phonograms Treaty") included a few important sections for those with interests in digital music. Full text of the bill can be found the U.S. Government's Thomas website. Section 103 prohibits the "circumvention of technological measures that control access to protected works; or manufacturing or trafficking in technology designed to circumvent measures that control access to, or protect rights of copyright owners in, such works." The bill implements into U.S. law all the specifics of the Performances and Phonograms Treaty.

The DCMA also establishes limited liability for:

- entities offering the transmission, routing, or providing of connections for digital online communications between points specified by a user of material of the user's choosing, without modification of the material; and
- providers of online services or network access.

Areas of U.S. law dealing with intellectual property and copyright in this "Digital World" were specified and strengthened with the passage of the DCMA.

The Internet poses quite a threat to copyright laws, especially in the areas of illegal music copying and distribution. It is very easy for millions of users to download information from other peoples' sites and in many cases this activity is not easily monitored. A user with a personal web page may also upload files to the server where the page is located and then allow other users to copy that file, regardless of the fact that it may be copyrighted.

Networks of computers also pose a problem when addressing copyright issues. Many university campuses, for example, have networks of student's personal computers. This network allows users to "share" files with the whole network, or with specific users by including a password. These shared files are stored on the individual computers, but can be accessed by any network user (as long as there is not a password). Most university campus computer users' shared files have revealed a large amount of MP3 files, the controversial audio format that transgresses copyright protections.

Motion Pictures Export Group (MP3)

MP3, audio layer 3, is simply a way of storing music in digital form. In 1988, the Moving Pictures Expert Group (MPEG) was formed in order to create a standard format for the compression and decompression (coded) of digital audio. The result was the standard MPEG1, a success for the creators, but a problem for the music industry. There are two main reasons why the MP3 format is causing problems for the music industry and copyrighted works-the rate and quality of the compression. The MPEG coded format has a 12-1 compression rate, which is the primary reason for related legal problems with MP3s. The compression allows for large sound files to be compressed into much smaller files that take up much less storage space and allows for quick up/downloading.

A 12 - 1 compression rate means that files, which may take up 36 megabytes of space, can be shrunk down to about 3 megabytes. It would be similar to a 120-page book that is compressed to only 10 pages, without any loss of quality. The key to the MP3 format is that when a file is compressed, it maintains its perceived sound quality. More than 15 years of research and development by the MPEG resulted in the technology that maintains sound quality with less space by stripping out overlapping waveforms. The relatively small file size allows users to easily store hundreds of MP3s on their hard drives as well as to add to their collection by downloading new files from the Internet or computers on a local network.

Once on a computer, a person needs an MP3 player to listen to the sound files. These players are available for downloading from the Internet. According to intellectual property laws, individuals who do not own the copyright to a work do not have the right to copy and distribute that work. Those who develop the technology did not think about copyright laws as an issue at the time, nor did the creators did not envision millions of computers with relatively huge storage capabilities all linked to one large network like the Internet.

One of the central questions raised by the issue of digital music is how copyright should be regulated and to what degree. There are multiple points of views with two extremes. One extreme is those interested in protecting intellectual property and copyright by any measures, and the other extreme are those who believe that the system is outdated and that the laws should be changed to reflect this different approach. Record companies usually fall into the former group, while music fans are in the latter. Those with a vested interest in copyright protection seem, for the most part, to be those who have monetary interests involved. With millions of dollars at stake for record companies, strong regulation is favored. Others, namely music fans, rejoice in the possibilities of the new technology.

Recording artists interests are understandably divided on the issue of technology. While the Internet can allow many people to listen to and become fans of an artist, it also allows for illegal distribution and copying of the artists' songs, resulting in a substantial loss of revenue for the artist. "Cyberspace poses unparalleled opportunities for the industry -- and unparalleled difficulties in copyright protection" (RIAA,1999). This quote, from part of the Recording Industry Association's web page, sums up the view of many of the record companies on technology.

The RIAA explains that the SDMI "will answer consumer demand for convenient accessibility to quality digital music, enable copyright protection for artists' work, and enable technology and music companies to build successful businesses" (RIAA,1999). The SDMI is still in the planning stages, but is on a "fast path toward expanding [the] digital music marketplace" (RIAA,1999). The SDMI has the support of not just record companies, but technology and business oriented companies. Included on the list of companies now involved with the SDMI talks are CDNow, Compaq Corp., Microsoft, Philips, Sanyo, Sony Electronics, Sun Microsystems, Texas Instruments, and Yamaha, among others, which illustrates the variety of companies who feel that there is a need for a standard for digital music distribution.

There are different ways of understanding the issue of the implications of globalization of information on intellectual property laws, and these derive from different ways of understanding the central concepts. The literature of recent years is replete with discussion of globalization and the growth of digital information and the influence these developments are having on domestic and international intellectual property regimes. A clear effect of globalization of information is a trend toward harmonization or standardization of intellectual property laws, in the direction of greater protection. Whereas this trend might appear to relate to positive economic effects, the literature of recent years suggests that these effects may be positive primarily for intellectual property producing nations and transnational corporations. It may also be diminishing the sovereignty of states in favor of the strength and power of private entities. It is possible that the prevalence of such writings in the literature is a response to the movement toward harmonization and stronger intellectual property protections-an attempt to ensure that some of the less heard voices are expressed (Nayyer, 2002).

III. Study Groundwork

A. WIPO-International Dimensions of eCommerce

This study also reviewed three areas in which the challenges from eCommerce have already had an impact, raising issues that implicate different sectors of legal interest. The three areas are electronic contracts, Internet jurisdiction and applicable laws, and the digital technology. In these three areas, the international dimensions of eCommerce complicate solutions and exercise caution against national interventions that would ignore potential cross-border impacts. While these subjects have significant importance for the Intellectual property field, they also have "horizontal" implications for other areas of law and policy, for example electronic contracts: paperless environment, the Internet: jurisdiction and applicable law, digital technology: enforcement and privacy.

1. Electronic Contracts: Paperless Environment

eCommerce raises questions concerning some of the new modalities used for achieving an offer and acceptance in the online environment. It places a premium on the clarity and transparency of the contractual terms and conditions, particularly as electronic contracts may involve parties from different parts of the world who may have had little or no interaction with each other apart from their communications online. Given these limitations, parties drafting contracts and those parties who would accept them, must be thoughtful about certain terms, such as disclaimers, choice of law and jurisdictional forum, and consumer protection. There are also limitations of liability issues and questions of mandatory local law. A failure to give these matters due regard may result in a surprising upset in the expectations of the parties.

With respect to contractual and evidentiary formalities, there is an increasing consensus that so long as an electronic communication has a sufficient measure of reliability, durability, and integrity to its content, no particular form or formal procedure is required in order to ensure its effectiveness for the purpose for which it is created. The model law provides that "[w]here the law requires information to be in writing, that requirement is met by a data message if the information contained therein is accessible so as to be usable for subsequent reference." With respect to a legal requirement that information be in "original form," this requirement is met if "there exists a reliable assurance as to the integrity of the information from the time when it was first generated in its final form, as a data message or otherwise."

Further, regarding a signature requirement, it is sufficient if the method used in an electronic communication to identify a person and indicate that person's approval of the information contained in the message "is as reliable as was appropriate for the purpose for which the data message was generated or communicated, in light of all the circumstances, including any relevant agreement."

The increasing recognition under the law of electronic means for contracting is an important step that facilitates the continuing development of electronic commerce. However, even when parties observe the requisite contractual principles and formalities in their online agreements, this does not guarantee that they have minimized their potential problems in contracts for the exploitation of intellectual property. As the following sections explain, questions of jurisdiction, applicable law and enforcement should be carefully considered – at the time of contracting – to bring added certainty, and where possible limit potential exposure, for businesses and consumers engaging in electronic commerce on global networks.

2. The Internet: Jurisdiction and Applicable Law

The Internet is multi-jurisdictional. Users can access the Internet from almost any place on earth. Because of packet-switching technology and the complex weave of digital networks and telecommunications infrastructure, digitized information may travel through various countries and jurisdictions, each with its own legal system, in order to reach its destination.

In light of the impact of this international medium on a world made up of separate countries, the jurisdictional issues loom large, especially in the context of intellectual property. These issues, however, extend beyond the precincts of intellectual property to implicate other areas, such as contracts (discussed above), fraud and tortuous behavior of all kinds, consumer protection, taxation, and the regulation of online content relating to obscenity and criminal law.

The following crosscutting issues arise in the context of private international law:

- Jurisdiction to adjudicate a dispute at a particular location (i.e., the forum or *sites*);
- the law applicable to the dispute (also referred to as choice of law or conflicts of law); and
- the recognition and enforcement of judgments in courts in foreign jurisdictions.

In eCommerce, these issues are complicated by the fact that one or more of the parties involved (or processes used) in the commercial activities – including Internet users, service and content providers, buyers, sellers, businesses (and their assets), technology systems and computer servers – may be located in different countries. Not only may uncertainty arise as to where the relevant activities are taking place, but the activities themselves may have intended and unintended consequences all over the globe, resulting in uncertainty when it comes to questions of localizing the dispute, determining the applicable law, and the practicalities of pursuing enforcement, or adequate dispute-settlement alternatives.

Owners of intellectual property seeking to manage their rights through licensing agreements, or to enforce them against infringement, are confronted with complex issues. In the case of a license to cover rights on the Internet, one must consider which laws in which countries may have a bearing on the agreement, including laws addressing electronic contracts, consumer protection, intellectual property, disclaimers and privacy aspects. In the case of rights holders seeking to enforce their rights, they will need to decide not only who (or what) to proceed against but also the proper forum, and under which applicable laws.

3. Digital Technology: Enforcement and Privacy

An important pillar of the intellectual property system consists of the provisions and mechanisms aimed at securing respect for the rights provided for by the law. Effective arrangements for the protection of these rights are crucial, as there is little point in establishing a detailed and comprehensive scheme for granting rights if mechanisms for their enforcement are lacking.

Historically, the question of the enforcement of intellectual property rights has been a difficult one and particularly in recent years, the issue has received increasing attention. A variety of factors in the past decade have contributed to a global upsurge in counterfeit and pirated goods: the dramatic increase in international trade, the dismantling of certain border controls, the difficulties experienced by national enforcement agencies in keeping up with the speed of developments and volume of traffic, and the formidable expansion of technologies. While it is difficult to measure with great accuracy the extent to which the problem is growing, it appears to have doubled since the end of the last decade.

The Internet generates new challenges in relation to issues of enforcement. All content converges into digital data on the Internet. Text, music, and images are reduced to strings of binary code. The digitization of data enables its transmission at speed in ephemeral form, but with the potential for indefinite storage in the memory of information technology and network devices. As a result, vast amounts of information and intellectual property are being transmitted in digital form to anyone with access to the network. These changes serve to accentuate the increasing need for speed in relation to the implementation and operation of enforcement measures that serve to put an end to infringements.

B. IITF 1995 Report-IP and NII

The Working Group on Intellectual Property Rights was established within the IITF to examine the intellectual property implications of the NII and to make recommendations on any appropriate changes to U.S. intellectual property law and policy. The IITF was established by President Clinton to articulate and implement the Administration's vision for the NII and to develop comprehensive telecommunications and information policies and programs to promote the development of the NII and best meet the country's needs.

The Report is based on the Working Group's Preliminary Draft (Green Paper), issued in July 1994, and on extensive public comment and testimony. In September 1994, the Working Group convened four days of hearings in three cities. In addition, more than 150 individuals and organizations-representing more than 425,000 members of the public, filed more than 1,500 pages of written comments in paper form and on the Internet. The open process instituted by the Working Group resulted in a well-developed, voluminous record reflecting the views of a broad spectrum of interested parties, including various electronic industries, telecommunications and information service providers, the academic, research, library and legal communities, and individual creators, copyright owners and users, as well as the computer software, motion picture, music, broadcasting, publishing, and other information and entertainment industries.

The Working Group examined the adequacy of the intellectual property laws to cope with the pace of technological change. It found that the patent, trademark, and trade secret laws need no adaptation at this time. It also found that the Copyright Act is fundamentally adequate and effective. In a few areas, however, it recommended limited amendments of the Copyright Act to take proper account of current technology. Technology has altered the copyright balance-in some instances, in favor of copyright owners and in others, in favor of users. The goal of the recommendations is to clarify existing law and adapt it where the balance has shifted.

The Report recommended that Section 106(3) of the Copyright Act be clarified to expressly recognize that copies or phonorecords of works may be distributed to the public by transmission, and that such transmissions fall within the exclusive distribution right of the copyright owner. The Report also recommended related amendments to the definitions of "transmit" and "publication," as well as distribution-related provisions regarding importation of copies or phonorecords.

The Working Group recommended that the library exemptions be amended to allow the preparation of three copies of works in digital format; to recognize that the use of a copyright notice on a published copy of a work is no longer mandatory; and to authorize the making of a limited number of digital copies by libraries and archives for purposes of preservation.

The Working Group further recommended that the Copyright Act be amended to provide an exemption for non-profit organizations to reproduce and distribute to the visually impaired-at cost-Braille, large type, audio or other editions of previously published literary works, provided that the owner of the exclusive right to distribute the work in the United States has not entered the market for such editions during the first year following first publication.

The Working Group recommended that the Copyright Act be amended to include a new Chapter 12, which would prohibit the importation, manufacture, or distribution of any device or product, or the provision of any service, the primary purpose or effect of which is to deactivate, without authority of the copyright owner or the law, any technological protections which prevent or inhibit the violation of exclusive rights under the copyright law.

The Working Group finally recommended that the Copyright Act be amended to prohibit the dissemination of copyright management information known to be false and the unauthorized removal or alteration of copyright management information. Copyright management information is defined as the name and other identifying information of the author of a work, the name and other identifying information of the copyright owner, terms and conditions for uses of the work, and information that the Register of Copyrights may prescribe by regulation ("Intellectual Property and the NII", U.S. Patent and Trademark Office, 1995).

C. Hardy's 1998 Report-Future of Copyright

The U.S. Copyright Office, Library of Congress, released a report titled "Project Looking Forward—Sketching the Future of Copyright in a Networked World." The report, commissioned from Professor I. Trotter Hardy, is part of a continuing effort by the Copyright Office to examine the future of the Internet and related digital communications technologies and to identify the legal and policy issues that might arise as a result.

The Internet and other digital technologies raise new issues for copyright law because they permit new ways of creating, using, and duplicating works of authorship. The report describes three "patterns" that arise as a copyright law confronts changing technology: new subject matter, new uses, and decentralized infringement. The report finds that decentralized infringement—where copies can be made cheaply and distributed widely by individuals, as is possible on the Internet—presents the most significant challenge today for copyright law's accommodation of new technologies. In spite of these challenges, the report concludes that copyright law has had a long history of adapting to technological advances, and that the possibilities of digital exploitation will not render copyright law obsolete.

The report presents a thorough explanation of the Internet as it works today, and describes how it will likely evolve. It then examines the legal issues raised by some of the features of digital technologies, such as Web posting, caching, and RAM copying. The report also addresses less commonly discussed issues. The report describes as "tomorrow's issues" such topics as non-public posting, protection of factual information on Web sites, Internet broadcasting, computer-generated works, and metered use of information.

The U.S. Copyright Office financed Professor Hardy's two-year study. In the 304-page report he mentioned that concern about a new technology's potential for mass copying, which he calls "decentralized infringement," is not a new phenomenon. He pointed out that technological or social change sometimes can bring about a situation where the "cost" of engaging in behavior defined as copyright infringement goes down. When that happens, the "incidence of the behavior goes up."

In the 19th century, for example, it was common for "hit-and-run" theater groups to travel to small towns in the United States and give unauthorized performances of plays. The technology of communications and transportation in those pre-telephone, pre-airplane days, Hardy wrote, "was such that it was hard for a rights organization in, say, New York, to learn of a traveling troupe performing for one or two days at a small town in the Midwest in time to do anything about it." Likewise, photocopy machines in the 1950s and 1960s and home audio- and videotape recordings beginning in the 1970s frustrated the ability of copyright holders to enforce their rights. How should the legal system respond to the challenge of new duplication methods? Hardy said the best answer is a "technological fix" that makes unauthorized copying more difficult. In the Internet realm, he said he favors the use of encryption, digital watermarks and other tools that foil would-be copiers, be they pirates or innocent but misguided Internet users. He also supports that the principles of current copyright law already enabling copyright owners to go after many net pirates and anyone who has substantially assisted them in making copies.

It is true that government could increase the penalties for unauthorized copying in an attempt to deter the mass behavior, or throw in the towel and declare certain copying activity lawful. "But I don't see the need to do those things," Hardy wrote, "because technology may change tomorrow" and a new, efficient preventive measure may become available.

If copyright owners cannot perfectly police the market, Hardy contended one could live with the leakage. "We live with a lot of decentralized infringement now -- just look at photocopying, for example," he wrote. The gap in enforcement provides an incentive to develop new technologies to trump infringers, he believes.

In researching his report, Hardy interviewed more than 80 corporate and government leaders involved with the Internet. That experience did more than help him to recommend a "go slow" approach to fiddling with copyright laws, he suggested. He also came away from the project with a healthy respect for the unknowable future. Indeed, the two lessons go hand in hand.

D. National Academies Press 2000 Report-Digital Dilemma

Late in 1997, the Computer Science and Telecommunications Board (CSTB) of the U.S. National Academies appointed a study committee to consider impacts that the emerging digital information infrastructure is having on intellectual property (IP) rights originating in the U.S. Constitution. In November 1999, this blue-ribbon committee released its report, "The Digital Dilemma: Intellectual Property in the Information Age by February 2000". This report presents the multiple facets of digitized intellectual property, defining terms, identifying key issues, and exploring alternatives. It follows the complex threads of law, business, incentives to creators, the American tradition of access to information, the international context, and the nature of human behavior. Technology is explored for its ability to transfer content and its potential to protect intellectual property rights.

"Information has increasingly become an event to be experienced, rather than an artifact to be kept," said committee chair Randall Davis, professor of Computer Science Department, Massachusetts Institute of Technology, Cambridge. The question of how to control distribution and use of digital information is much more than a legal issue alone. Law, business, and technology all interact, hence approaching the problem from a single viewpoint will be inadequate. Many stakeholders are affected; anyone with an interest in eCommerce will feel the consequences of the decisions made on this topic.

Digital intellectual property and the information infrastructure are prompting a re-examination of the first-sale rule, which says that the initial sale of a copy of a work exhausts the copyright owner's right to control further distribution. Thus, an individual, a library, or other entity is free to give away, lend, rent, or sell its copies of books. But in the digital environment, consistent implementation of the rule has become more complex. Because of the pervasive reach of electronic networks, a single copy of a work available from a digital library could diminish the market for the work much more than if it were distributed only in hard copy. Maintaining the limited degree of access to published materials that was established for hard-copy versions of information must continue in the digital environment, the report declares.

Information providers are using licensing provisions and technical protection services to manage access. Licensing is commonly used to provide access to some types of digital information such as software, and more recently is being applied to research journals and scientific databases. This practice is stirring controversy because access expires after a predetermined length of time. The issue is particularly important with mass-market licenses-for example, "shrink wrap" licenses for software and other products-which offer no opportunity to negotiate terms. Licenses are contracts, and thus are under no obligation to include the important elements of public policy found in copyright law, such as fair use. If these types of licenses come into widespread use for content distribution, contract law will potentially become a widespread substitute for copyright law, according to the report. That would imply a change in the balance of private ownership and public access associated with copyright.

Some technical protection services offer the owners of digital information some assurance that distributing a single copy of a digital work does not result in uncontrollable dissemination by making it difficult for consumers to save or print it. The committee concluded, however, that this may have adverse effects on accessing and preserving our permanent social and cultural heritage, since digitized material could easily be withdrawn from circulation.

Given the availability of alternative mechanisms that offer most of the advantages and far fewer risks than electronic distribution, not every information product should be distributed by digital networks, as stated in the report. High-value, long-lived products, such as classic movies like "The Wizard of Oz," may never be made legally available on the Internet while protected under copyright, because the consequences of an individual capturing the movie in digital form are too great. The technical, legal, and social enforcement costs of ensuring that this does not happen are also prohibitive.

E. International Copyright Treaties and the Role of the United States

11. History of the International Framework

There is no standard international copyright law rather, an international system which sets norms for protection based on national laws. Several international treaties link together the major trading nations and establish minimum standards for the protection of copyrighted works. The situation is complicated due to the existence of two differing, major legal traditions (such as common law and civil law) applicable to what are regarded as copyrighted works.

The countries, that follow common law, or the Anglo-American, legal tradition, have developed copyright systems in which the principal focus is on promoting the creation of new works for the public's benefit by protecting the author's economic rights. The underlying theory is grounded on the premise that providing economic incentives will in turn lead to the creation of even more works, which in turn will rebound to the public benefit.

Countries that follow civil *law* tradition tend to view the copyright created as part of an author's natural human rights, or part of one's right of personality. Thus, under this system, the protection of an author's moral rights is as essential as the corresponding protection of his/her economic rights. Additional protections afforded by these moral rights, include, but are not limited to, the right to be named as the author of the work and the right to prevent uses of the work that may bring discredit or dishonor upon the author's reputation.

2. The International Copyright Treaties

In order to understand the obligations of the United States under the existing international copyright treaties, it is necessary to discuss them from the accession and implementation of each applicable treaty.

3. The Universal Copyright Convention

The first significant copyright treaty that the United States acceded to and ratified was the Universal Copyright Convention (UCC), in 1971. A less rigorous version of the Berne Convention was adopted by UCC. The appeal of the UCC was limited primarily to those countries, in particular the U.S. and the former Soviet Union, that desired a means of protecting copyright holder's interests overseas, but they did not wish to subscribe to the provisions of the Berne Convention.

The primary benefit of the UCC is its requirement that members of the Convention apply national treatment principals to their domestic laws. These national treatment principals require that foreign nationals be treated the same as domestic citizens for purposes of copyright protection.

The existence of major drawbacks to the UCC eventually led to the search for a more rigorous means of enforcing U.S. copyrights by other treaties. These drawbacks included: (1) the lack of countries belonging to the UCC; (2) few protective requirements beyond national treatment (countries with weak national copyright laws afforded little or no protection to U.S. nationals); and, (3) lack of enforcement mechanisms (the UCC was administered primarily by the United Nations Educational, Scientific and Cultural Organization (UNESCO), from which the United States had withdrawn due to unrelated political reasons).

4. The Berne Convention

In an effort to cure the perceived limitations of the UCC, primarily by greatly expanding the geographic scope but by also taking advantage of the significantly stricter minimum standards of protection, the United States entered into the Berne Convention in 1988. Joining Berne did not require any extensive modification of existing U.S. copyright law, since the Copyright Act of 1976 had already removed or provided for the expiration of those provisions which Congress had determined were incompatible with the requirements of the Berne Convention.

The major limitation of Berne, as perceived by some members of the world community, including the U.S., was its lack of enforcement provisions. Enforcement and administration of the Berne provisions were in the hands of the World Intellectual Property Organization (WIPO). WIPO is a specialized agency of the United Nations whose primary purpose is to promote the protection of intellectual property rights and is responsible for the administration of a multitude of intellectual property treaties. Proceedings before the WIPO were based on consultation and consensus, which had previously proven to be ineffective as a means to settle disputes. While the U.S. had acquired much stronger international rights, for its own copyright holders, the ability to enforce treaty obligations gathered from the Berne Convention through the WIPO was perceived seen as a weak link.

5. The TRIPs Agreement and the GATT/WTO

Although some progress was clearly being made in an effort to protect copyrights internationally, it was conceived that the enforcement mechanism could be made substantially more forceful by tying it to existing multilateral treaties such as the GATT.

The U.S. copyright industry was by that point a significant factor in reducing our balance of payments deficit. In fact, by the end of the Uruguay Round of negotiations concluded in 1993, it was estimated that the copyright industry reduced that deficit by over $45 billion. However, losses to the industry from piracy and trade barriers were estimated by the industry at between $15 to $17 billion annually. Obviously, it was in the United States' interest to improve protection for copyrights, thereby improving the balance of payments.

This goal was achieved during the Uruguay Round of the Multilateral Trade Negotiations on the GATT. The Uruguay round, not only established the WTO to co-administer the GATT, along with the WIPO, but expanded the provisions of the GATT to not only regulate the trade of goods, but of services, and the "trade-related aspects of intellectual property rights" (TRIPs). The ability to enforce these provisions, which had proven so elusive in the past, was immediately reinforced by the other major achievement of the Uruguay Round, the new Understanding on Dispute Settlement Procedures (DSU). Prior to the creation of TRIPs, and while administered solely by the WIPO, the only mechanism for settling disputes, besides consultation and consensus, required that disputes be taken before the International Court of Justice. This provision was illusory, as no dispute was ever taken to the Court in the over 45 years prior to the Uruguay Round. The new GATT/WTO based mechanism for settling disputes will be covered in greater detail later in this paper.

The TRIPs agreement itself was based on the intellectual property chapter of the North American Free Trade Agreement (NAFTA). The 1992 NAFTA agreement, between Canada, Mexico, and the U.S. contained an extensive intellectual property chapter, which provided for "Berne-plus" obligations on all the parties.

Some have suggested that perhaps the most important compromise reached during the TRIPs negotiations related to the acceptance of GATT jurisdiction and the establishment of minimal standards for intellectual property protection. These new minimal standards included the recognition of "national treatment" and transparency as a cornerstone for international copyright protection and the reliance upon the Berne Convention for most of the substantive copyright standards. In fact, Article 9 of the TRIPs agreement requires all members of GATT/WTO to comply with Articles 1 through 21 of the Berne Convention. Also included in the TRIPs agreement was a transition mechanism, which takes into account the differences between the developed and less developed nations.

Even the new TRIPs provisions are deemed by some to be flawed. Most of the criticism has focused on size of the intellectual property staff within the WTO, which by 1995 numbered only three. This contrasted with the intellectual property staff of WIPO, which numbered over 500. Another criticism has focused on the very nature of the "member only" policy of the dispute settlement process of the WTO. That is, only sovereign states, which make up the WTO as members, are afforded rights under the dispute settlement process, thus precluding any possibility of the right of private action on the part of the actual copyright holder. Those who have a direct interest in protecting their intellectual property rights may be at the whim of their own government who may or may not be responsive to their interest.

6. The WIPO Treaties

In December 1996, two new copyright treaties were signed in Geneva: the WIPO Copyright Treaty and the WIPO Performances and Phonograms Treaty. By October 1998, Congress enacted the Digital Millennium Copyright Act (DMCA), which implemented these two copyright treaties. Some believed that the existing U.S. Copyright Law met or surpassed most of the WIPO treaties' requirements. U.S. law did require some adaptation to comply with provisions relating to digital creation, communication, and exploitation.

The WIPO treaties, however, only go into effect after ratification by at least 30 countries. The U.S. became only the ninth country to have ratified the agreement as of September 17, 1999, even though over 50 countries were signatories to the treaty. Thus, at this time, these treaties are not in effect and play no part in the immediate controversy.

7. The Dispute Settlement Process under GATT/WTO

A dispute settlement process existed under GATT 1947, but it had no fixed timetables, rulings were relatively easy to block, and many cases dragged on inconclusively. Thus, as mentioned previously, the Dispute Settlement Understanding (DSU) was created during the Uruguay Round of GATT. The new system has been described as a coherent and self-contained legal framework to which all member countries have agreed, thereby excluding any further legal action in a context outside the WTO.

The new DSU created a standing Dispute Settlement Body (DSB) to oversee the application of the process. The DSB has the authority to among, other things establish panels, adopt panel and appellate body reports (decisions), oversee the implementation of panel recommendations, and authorize retaliation.

The outline of the process provided by the International Trade Center (ITC), is set out below. (The ITC is a technical cooperation organization, which exists as a subsidiary organ of both the WTO and the United Nations Conference on Trade and Development (UNCTAD)):

- Initially, the complaining country will request and hold bilateral consultations with the country concerning the measure in question; these consultations are aimed at finding a mutually acceptable solution to the problem.

- If the consultations fail, the WTO Dispute Settlement Body (DSB) will, upon request, establish a panel of (normally three) independent experts whose task it is to examine the case, hear the arguments of the two sides, and present a report to the DSB stating whether any rights of the complaining party have been violated or impaired.

- The DSB will normally adopt the report, including any recommendations for action which the panel may have formulated, unless one (or both) of the parties to the dispute makes an appeal to the WTO Appellate Body, examine any issue of law contained in the panel report and submit its own report to the DSB.

- After the adoption of the report by the DSB of the panel or the Appellate Body, the DSB will monitor the implementation of any recommendations made, e.g., to withdraw the measure, which has been found to be violating the rights of the complaining country.

- If corrective action is not taken within a reasonable period of time, the violating country will be obliged to provide compensation to the affected country, e.g. through tariff reductions in areas of particular interest to the complainant.

- If no satisfactory compensation is agreed, the complaining country can request from the DSB authorization for retaliatory action through the suspension of concessions or obligations against the other party.

As a general rule, if a case runs its full course to a first ruling, the time frame is about one year, about 15 months if appealed. At any point in the process the issue may be resolved through mediation and consultation. As an alternative means of dispute settlement, members may seek arbitration within the WTO framework. This is allowable where: (1) the issues in conflict are "clearly defined by both parties" to the dispute; (2) the parties agree to submit to arbitration and the procedures to be followed; (3) all members are given prior notice of the arbitration (third parties may join in the arbitration only with the consent of the original parties); and (4) the parties must agree to abide by the arbitration award.

8. Enforcement Provisions of the DSU

It has been noted that WTO rules, like the preceding GATT rules, are simply not "binding" in the traditional sense. When a panel issues a ruling adverse to a member, there is no prospect of incarceration, injunctive relief, and damages for harm inflicted or police enforcement. The WTO has no jailhouse, no bail bondsman, no blue helmets, no truncheons or tear gas. Rather, the WTO—essentially a confederation of sovereign national governments—relies upon voluntary compliance. The genius of the GATT/WTO system is the flexibility with which it accommodates the national exercise of sovereignty, yet promotes compliance with its trade rules through incentives.

However, the WTO, through the DSU, is not without enforcement mechanisms, even if they are technically voluntary. The reliability of the DSU as a means of not only securing a judgment, but as a means of securing compliance with GATT/WTO provisions is a significant element of the ongoing importance of the GATT itself. The DSU exhorts members to comply noting, prompt compliance with recommendations or rulings of the DSB is essential in order to ensure effective resolution of disputes to the benefit of all members.

The implementation plan of a panel or Appellate Body decision under the DSU has been characterized as a three-phase process. The first phase is the acceptance of the plan for implementation: If a panel or Appellate Body report finds that a member has acted in a manner inconsistent with its WTO obligations or impairs or nullifies obligations under article XXIII of the GATT, it requires that member to notify the DSB of its plan for implementing the report at a DSB meeting held within 30 days after the report is adopted. If it is impracticable to comply immediately with the recommendations and rulings, the member shall have a "reasonable period of time" in which to do so.

The second phase deals with the monitoring of the implementation period: the DSU allows the winning complainant mechanisms to compel a losing members compliance with a panel decision. These mechanisms include a request to the original panel to review the implementation or to actively monitor the losing members implementation of the decision.

The third phase concerns the idea of compensation and retaliation. If a losing party does not implement the panel's recommendation or ruling within a reasonable period of time, the winning member may seek compensation. If such compensation is requested, the losing party is required to enter into consultations to develop mutually acceptable compensation. If no satisfactory agreement is reached, the complainant may request authorization from the DSB to suspend concessions or other obligations under the covered agreements due the losing member. In fact, if no agreement is reached within 30 days of the end of the "reasonable period", it is required that the DSB approve such measures.

It is important to remember that the system is voluntary in nature and that it up to the losing party to decide how to respond. Losing members may choose to comply by: (1) implementing the recommendations and rulings; (2) providing compensation; or (3) accepting the suspension of concessions by the winning party(ies). However, the preferred means of implementing panel decisions is by the full implementation of the panel decision to bring the offending measure into conformity with the covered agreements, rather than by compensation or the suspension of concessions.

F. Online Business Models

eCommerce gives rise to new kinds of business models. But the Web is also likely to reinvent tried-and-true models. Auctions are a perfect example. One of the oldest business models, auctions have been widely used throughout the world to set prices for such items as agricultural commodities, financial instruments, and unique items like fine art and antiquities. Companies like eBay have popularized the auction model and broadened its application on the web to a wide array of goods and services. Business models are categorized in different ways. Presently, there is no single, comprehensive, and cogent taxonomy of Web business models one can point to. Some of the generic forms of business models observable on the Web include: brokerage, advertising, infomediary, merchant, manufacturer, affiliate, community, subscription, and utility. These models are implemented in a variety of ways as explained in types of models below. Moreover, any given firm may combine different models as part of its Web business strategy. Thus, an advertising model may be blended with a subscription model to yield an overall strategy that is profitable. The taxonomy proposed is not meant to be exhaustive or definitive. Business models on the Web evolve rapidly. New and interesting variations may be expected in the future (Rappa, 2001).

Business models have taken on greater importance in the last few years in the realm of intellectual property. Within the legal community, business models (or more broadly speaking, "business methods") have fallen increasingly within the context of law. Some of the most common current Internet business models that are relevant to this study include (Rappa, 2001):

1. Brokerage Model Brokers are market-makers: they bring buyers and sellers together and facilitate transactions. These may be business-to-business (B2B), business-to-consumer (B2C), or consumer-to-consumer (C2C) markets. A broker makes its money by charging a fee or commission for each transaction it enables. Brokerage models may take a number of different forms, such as:

Buy/Sell Fulfillment-Customers place buy and sell orders for a particular product or service. The broker charges the buyer and/or seller a transaction fee. Some models work on volume and low overhead to deliver the best-negotiated prices (Orbitz, CarsDirect, Respond.com).

Market Exchange-Common model in B2B markets. In the exchange model, the broker typically charges the seller a transaction fee based on the value of the sale. The pricing mechanism can be a simple offer/buy, offer/negotiated buy, or an auction offer/bid approach (ChemConnect.com, World Chemical Exchange).

Business Trading Community-or "Vertical web community," a concept pioneered by VerticalNet. A site that acts as a "source of information and dialogue for a particular vertical market," VerticalNet's communities contain product information in buyers' guides, supplier and product directories, daily industry news and articles, job listings, and classifieds. In addition, VerticalNet's sites enable B2B exchanges of information, supplementing existing trade shows and trade association activities.

Demand Collection System-The "name-your-price" business model pioneered by Priceline. Prospective buyer makes a final (binding) bid for a specified good or service, and the broker seeks fulfillment. The broker's fee is the spread between the bid and fulfillment price and perhaps a processing charge (Priceline.com).

Distributor-A catalog-type operation that connects a large number of product manufacturers with volume and retail buyers. Broker facilitates business transactions between franchised distributors and their trading partners. For buyers, it enables faster time to market and time to volume as well as reducing the cost of procurement. By providing the buyer with a means of retrieving quotes from preferred distributors-showing buyer-specific prices, lead-time, and recommended substitutions-transaction are more efficient. For distributors, it decreases the cost of sales by performing quoting, order processing, tracking order status, and changes more quickly and with less labor (Questlink.com, ConvergeTrade.com).

Virtual Mall-A site hosts many online merchants. The Mall typically charges setup, monthly listing, and/or per transaction fees. The virtual mall model may be most effectively realized when combined with a generalized portal. Also, more sophisticated malls will provide automated transaction services and relationship marketing opportunities (ChoiceMall.com).

Metamediary-A business that brings buyers and online merchants together and provides transaction services such as financial settlement and quality assurance. It is a virtual mall, but one that will process the transaction, track orders, and provide billing and collection services. The metamediary protects consumers by assuring satisfaction with merchants. The metamediary charges a setup fee and a fee per transaction (HotDispatch.com).

Auction Broker-A site that conducts auctions for sellers (individuals or merchants). Broker charges the seller a fee, which is typically scaled with the value of the transaction. Seller takes highest bid(s) from buyers above a minimum. Auctions can vary in terms of the offering and bidding rules. Reverse auctions are a common variant (eBay.com).

Classifieds-A listing of items for sale or wanted for purchase, typically run by local news content providers. Price may or may not be specified. Listing charges are incurred regardless of whether a transaction occurs (Monster.com, Match.com).

Search Agent-An agent (i.e., an intelligent software agent or "robot") used to search-out the price and availability for a good or service specified by the buyer, or to locate hard to find information. (MySimon.com, DealTime.com).

Bounty Broker-The offer of a reward (usually a significant monetary sum) for finding a person, thing, idea, or other desired, but hard to find item. The broker may list items for a flat fee and a percent of the reward, if the item is successfully found (BountyQuest.com).

Transaction Broker-Provides a third-party mechanism for buyers and sellers to settle payment for a transaction (PayPal.com, Escrow.com).

2. Advertising Model The web advertising model is an extension of the traditional media broadcast model. The broadcaster, in this case, a web site, provides content (usually, but not necessarily, for free) and services (like e-mail, chat, forums) mixed with advertising messages in the form of banner ads. The banner ads may be the major or sole source of revenue for the broadcaster. The broadcaster may be a content creator or a distributor of content created elsewhere. The advertising model only works when the volume of viewer traffic is large or highly specialized. Advertising models may take a number of different forms, such as:

Generalized Portal-High-volume traffic driven by generic or diversified content or services. The high volume makes advertising profitable and permits further diversification of site services (Yahoo.com).

Personalized Portal-The generic nature of a generalized portal undermines user loyalty. This has led to the creation of portals that allow customization of the interface and content. This increases loyalty through the user's own time investment in personalizing the site. (MyYahoo.com).

Specialized Portal -- Also called a vertical portal. Here volume is less important than a well-defined user demographic. For example, a site that attracts homebuyers, or new parents, can be highly sought after as a venue for certain advertisers who are willing to pay a premium to reach that particular audience (iVillage.com).

Query-based Paid Placement-Selling favorable link positioning (i.e., sponsored links) or advertising keyed to particular search terms in a user query, such as Overture's trademarked "pay-for-performance" model (Google.com, Overture.com).

Contextual Advertising-Freeware developers who bundle advertising with their product. For example, a browser extension that automates authentication and form fill-ins, also delivers advertising links or pop-ups as the user surfs the web. Contextual advertisers can sell targeted advertising based on an individual user's surfing behavior (Gator.com, eZula.com).

3. Infomediary Model-Data about consumers and their consumption habits are valuable, especially when that information is carefully analyzed and used to target marketing campaigns. Some firms are able to function as infomediaries by collecting and selling information. Infomediary models may take a number of different forms, such as:

Advertising Networks-A service that feeds banner ads to a network of sites, thereby enabling advertisers to deploy large marketing campaigns. By using cookies, the Ad Network operator collects data on web users that can be used to analyze marketing effectiveness (DoubleClick.com).

Audience Measurement Services -- online audience market research agencies (Nielsen//Netratings.com).

Registration-Content-based sites that are free to view but require users to register (other information may or may not be collected). Registration allows inter-session tracking of users' site usage patterns and thereby generates data of greater potential value in targeted advertising campaigns. This is the most basic form of infomediary model. (NYTimes.com). Registration models may take a number of different forms, such as:

Incentive Marketing -- The customer loyalty program model. Provides incentives to customers such as redeemable points or coupons for making purchases from associated retailers. Data collected about users are sold for the purpose of target marketing. (Coolsavings.com, MyPoints.com, Greenpoints.com).

4. Merchant Model Wholesalers and retailers of goods and services. Sales may be made based on list prices or through auction. In some cases, the goods and services may be unique to the web and not have a traditional "brick-and-mortar" storefront. Merchant models may take a number of different forms, such as:

<u>Virtual Merchant</u>-A business that operates only over the Web, also known as "pure-play e-tailers" (Amazon.com).

<u>Catalog Merchant</u> The migration of mail-order to a Web-based order business (LandsEnd.com).

<u>Click and Mortar</u>-Traditional brick-and-mortar retail establishment with Web storefront. (Barnes & Noble.com).

<u>Bit Vendor-</u>A merchant that deals strictly in digital products and services and, in its purest form, conducts both sales and distribution over the web (Eyewire.com).

5. Manufacturer Model A model predicated on the power of the web to allow a manufacturer (i.e., a company that creates a product or service) to reach buyers directly and thereby compress the distribution channel. The manufacturer model can be based on efficiency, improved customer service, or a better understanding of customer preferences. (<u>Apple Computer</u>). Manufacturer models may take a number of different forms, such as:

<u>Brand Integrated Content</u>-Traditionally, manufacturers rely on advertising to build customer awareness. Commericals via broadcasters like radio, television and mass market publishers (newspapers and magazines), or through product placement in TV and motion pictures, have been a mainstay of modern business. The Web enables a manufacturer to integrate their brand more intimately with the content. The innovator in this respect is the luxury automobile maker, BMW. The company's bmwfilms.com is a creative blend of advertising with entertainment that paves the way for a new approach that might be called "advertainment"-taking the idea of product placement advertising to the extreme.

6. Affiliate Model In contrast to the generalized portal, which seeks to drive a high volume of traffic to one site-the affiliate model-provides purchase opportunities wherever people may be surfing. It does this by offering financial incentives (in the form of a percentage of revenue) to affiliated partner sites. The affiliates provide purchase-point click-through to the merchant. It is a pay-for-performance model-if an affiliate does not generate sales, it represents no cost to the merchant. The affiliate model is inherently well-suited to the Web, which explains its popularity. Variations include banner exchange, pay-per-click, and revenue sharing programs (Barnes & Noble.com, Amazon.com).

7. Community Model The viability of the community model is based on user loyalty. Users have a high investment of both time and emotion in the site. In some cases, users are regular contributors of content and/or money. Having users who visit continually offers advertising, infomediary or specialized portal opportunities. The community model may also run on a subscription fee for premium services.

Voluntary Contributor-Similar to the traditional public broadcasting model-the listener or viewer contributor method is used in not-for-profit radio and television broadcasting. The model is predicated on the creation of a community of users who support the site through voluntary donations. Not-for-profit organizations may also seek funding from charitable foundations and corporate sponsors that support the organization's mission. The web holds great potential as a contributor based model because the user base is more readily apparent. (The Classical Station, (WCPE.org)). Voluntary contributor models can take a number of different forms, such as:

Knowledge Networks-or Expert sites, that provide a source of information based on professional expertise or the experience of other users. Sites are typically run like a forum where persons seeking information can pose questions and receive answers from (presumably) someone knowledgeable about the subject. The experts may be employed staff, a regular cadre of volunteers, or in some cases simply anyone on the Web who wishes to respond (AllExperts.com).

8. Subscription Model Users pay a periodic-daily, monthly, or annual-subscriber fee to gain access to the service. It is not uncommon for sites combine free content with "premium" (i.e., subscriber-only) content. Subscribers pay for a service without respect to actual usage rates (Classmates.com, Listen.com).

9. Utility Model The utility model is based on metering usage or a "pay as you go" approach. Unlike subscriber services, metered services are based on actual usage rates. Traditionally, metering has been used for essential services (e.g., electricity water, long-distance telephone services). Internet service providers (ISPs) in some parts of the world operate as utilities, charging customers for connection minutes, as opposed to the subscriber model common in the U.S.

IV. Chapter Summary

As a consequence of the fast development of information technologies, and especially the Internet, many new types of transactions have been developed in recent years. Before the Internet, several kinds of business transactions were normally carried out by telephone, telex, and by fax. However, it was not until the development of a network that could transfer vast amounts of information together with interactive features and with the digital capacity for making high quality copies that the term eCommerce could be properly used. The Internet, together with the use, convergence, and improvement of new technologies, is creating new challenges and opportunities. As demonstrated in this chapter, the reference to the use of these technologies, online business models, treaties, and the existing legal framework for the manufacture and exportation of goods and services are among these challenges and opportunities.

The relationship between intellectual property rights and eCommerce may be identified in two specific areas. The first is the appropriate and predictable legal environment that a balanced IP regime could bring to the progress and expansion of eCommerce activities. The second area applies to the intellectual property content that may be transmitted or delivered through the Internet and become the object of eCommerce. The relationship between eCommerce and IP copyrights is relatively new. The IP regime is becoming an extensive legal monopoly to protect capital investment rather than a system designed to promote innovation, creativity, and inventiveness. The rights of authors, inventors, and users of IP have been losing ground and weight in the intellectual property rights system. The bibliography of the literature reviewed is attached in Appendix A.

The issues associated with intellectual property in digital form raised by several authors in this chapter are difficult and challenging. In order to address the issues, a broad qualitative research methodological approach, content analysis procedures, is designed to acquire the desired data for analysis and interpretation, and is discussed in the next chapter, Research Methodology and Data Collections.

Chapter 3: Research Methodology & Data Collection

I. Introduction:

Researchers are exploring appropriate research approaches and methodologies in analyzing the digital economy (Kim; Barau; Whinston; 2001). The research domain of eCommerce is particularly challenging, because of the evolving nature of definitions, and the volatility of the phenomena (Clarke, 2000). The research methodology for this study drew upon content analysis research procedures and applied them to intellectual property copyright laws and regulations. This chapter consists of the description of research method, data collection, and organization and analysis processes used for testing the research hypothesis, exploring research questions and constructing theory.

II. Qualitative Research Methodology

Qualitative research involved non-quantitative methods of data collection and analysis (Lofland & Lofland 1984). It focuses on quality, a term referring to the essence or ambience of something (Berg 1989). The study involves a subjective methodology and the researcher as the research instrument (Adler & Adler 1987). Many researchers state that all inquiry starts in a qualitative form (Lauer & Asher, 1988). Some qualitative researchers argue that, an objective approach to studying human events---is neither desirable nor, perhaps, even possible (Eisner, 1998; Wolcott, 1994). Most qualitative researchers assert that different individuals may hold multiple perspectives, with each perspective having equal validity, or truth (Creswell, 1998).

The qualitative research methodology is based on description, interpretation, narrative verification and evaluation (Peshkin, 1993). In the present study the researcher's ability to interpret and make sense of what was observed was critical for an understanding of a social phenomenon, intellectual property copyright law. In this sense, the researcher is an instrument in much the same way that a sociogram, rating scale, or intelligence test is an instrument for other researchers (Leedy & Ormord, 2001).

A detailed and systematic examination of the contents of intellectual property copyright laws and regulations was conducted for the purpose of identifying patterns and themes for adjustments in the US legal system to respond to the new technological environment in effective and appropriate ways. Content analysis is useful for examining trends and patterns reflected in documents. It provides an empirical basis for monitoring shifts in public opinion (Stemler and Bebell 1998). Content Analysis is the systematic assessing and interpreting of the form and substance of communication (Rosenberg and Oxman; 1990). Perhaps due to the fact that it can be applied to any piece of writing or occurrence of recorded communication, content analysis is currently used in a wide variety of fields, including marketing and media studies, literature and rhetoric, ethnography and cultural studies, gender and age issues, sociology, political science, psychology and cognitive science. Content analysis identifies the intentions, foci or communication trends of individuals, groups or institutions (Berelson, 1952).

Roberts (1994) argue that the goal of understanding a phenomenon from the point of view of the participants and its particular social and institutional context is largely lost when textual data are quantified. Qualitative content analysis uses the methodological strength of content analysis, based upon communication research for systematic analysis of large amounts of textual material, and elaboration on the qualitative steps of analysis (Krippendorff, 1980).

According to Krippendorff (1980), six questions must be addressed in every content analysis as employed in the study: 1) Which data are analyzed? 2) How are they defined?

The specific data collected 3) What is the population from which they are drawn? 4) What is the context relative to which the data are analyzed? 5) What are the boundaries of the analysis? 6) What is the target of the inferences? These steps are clearly described and addressed in the following sections.

In researching qualitative content analysis techniques for gathering information, three inter-related procedures were found to be an appropriate and effective method to obtain and analyze the specific data desired. First, academic literature was reviewed on the topic of intellectual property copyright laws and business models. Second, the research design relied on information provided by US government commerce Policy Web site (US Department Of Commerce, doc.gov), US Copyright Office Web site (Library of Congress, loc.gov), World Intellectual Property Organization Web site (WIPO, wipo.org), and Word Trade Organization Web site (WTO, wto.org). Third, surveys, current Internet industry reports, and IP related court cases were reviewed. These sources represent the collection of related trade publication articles and press releases. The relative contexts to which the data are analyzed are the current copyright laws and regulations and suggestions for future research for intellectual property copyright. The boundaries of the analysis are restricted to the copyright laws and regulations and did not include the domain names, trademarks and patents. The targets of the inferences were directed towards copyright stakeholders—congress, industries, citizens and society. The data was gathered and organized using the following structure:

i. Phase One - Data Collection:

This section discusses the definition of the data: primary and secondary data. The areas discussed are the collection, design of the data and the strategy utilized for collection:

a. Primary Data:

The primary data was collected using published literature, articles and the Internet specific publications, the Internet itself, trade journals and newspapers for testing research hypothesis, exploring research questions and building theory. Additional research information was obtained by the researcher's daily eCommerce graduate teaching experience at the School of Business and Information Management, National University.

b. Secondary Data:

The secondary data was collected through surveys, and IP copyright court cases for analysis and interpretation of the study. The Survey.Net collected the secondary data utilized for this study by means of a survey of typical consumers. The target audience of the survey and the population from which the data are drawn is typical in the sense that they were not selected based on any particular demographic criteria.

c. Research Instrument:

The World Wide Web and the researcher served as the research instruments. The focus of the questions in the survey was the participant's opinion on the 'property rights in the cyberspace'. The data gathered via the research survey was critical in support of the analysis and findings of the study.

B. Phase Two: Testing Research Hypothesis

eCommerce has created an exciting prospect. For the first time the author, publisher, or reader, are able to communicate instantaneously. The opportunities for learning about customer appeal, critical analysis, and improving one's publication, for example, without having the time delay that comes from waiting for the first printing to be sold out have become possible.

One of the fundamental questions posed in the sub-problems section in chapter 1 was: Should an individual who is browsing information offered on the Internet be required to obtain the author's permission before viewing the information, saving the information on disk, or printing it for future reading, even if there is no intention to infringe on the author's copyrights? When an author's work is on-line, it becomes available to individuals and allows listening, viewing, copying, and printing of the journal for example, in its entirety or only specific articles. Either an infringement has taken place because there is a distribution of the author's work that the author has not authorized, or there has been no infringement because the downloading by the individual is no different from the reading or photocopying of the journal, which an individual could do in a library.

While the author desires the rewards that come from his or her creation, the public desires as much access to the author's work as possible. Copyright law gives protection to authors as an incentive to create, but it also limits the extent of that protection so as to page that was found on the infringer, with half of the total amount going to the owner and the other half going to the government.

In 1897, criminal copyright infringement was implemented into copyright law. Infringement violations hinged on commercial exploitation. The Copyright Act of 1909 sought to codify the principles of the Copyright Clause, but over time it became unworkable because the statute did not account for the development of technology, specifically the use of the Internet and its impact on copyrighted works. Thus, the Copyright Acts of 1976 amended copyright law to a willful and purposeful use of works that resulted in commercial advantage or private financial gain.

The courts interpreted this to require that an infringer need only have intended to receive a commercial advantage or financial gain even if there was no actual advantage or gain. In 1980, the Copyright Act was amended to protect original works of authorship fixed in any tangible medium of expression, now known or later developed, from which they can be perceived, reproduced, or otherwise communicated, either directly or with the aid of a machine or device. The effect was that Copyright law would now protect the expression of an idea but not the idea itself.

The continual increase of infringement activity persuaded the U.S. Congress to establish felony penalties for all categories of copyright infringement under the Copyright Felony Act of 1992 by increasing penalties up to a $250,000 fine and/or up to five years in prison. A defense to copyright infringement is the Doctrine of Fair Use. The defense permits the infringement of a copyright owner's exclusive rights if certain conditions are met. The Copyright Act lists four factors to be considered in determining whether or not a use is fair:

1. the purpose and character of the use, including whether such use is of a commercial nature or is for nonprofit educational purposes;

2. the nature of the copyrighted work;

3. the amount and substantiality of the portion used in relation to the copyrighted work as a whole; and

4. the effect of the use upon the potential market for or value of the copyrighted work.

The fourth factor by way of commercial use of a copyrighted work usually cuts against a determination of fair use by the infringer. The Berne Convention for the Protection of Literary and Artistic Works deals with copyrights on the international level. In 1989, Congress joined the other 135 member countries by amending the Copyright Act to provide reciprocal enforcement of copyrights between countries. The Berne Convention provides authors with internationally recognized rights including reproduction, conversion, and other forms of communication to the public. However, the Berne Convention failed to provide ways to enforce those rights.

These rights were resolved by the Agreement on Trade-Related Aspects of Intellectual Property Rights, (TRIPS Agreement), in 1995 following the Uruguay Round negotiations and the creation of the World Trade Organization. The TRIPS Agreement incorporated the provisions of the Berne Convention and provided enforcement devices which participating countries must make available to copyright owners.The World Intellectual Property Organization, (WIPO) Treaties, signed in 1996, provided further remedies for copyright owners to enforce their rights internationally.

In 1993, President Clinton formed the Information Infrastructure Task Force to study the issues of copyright and use of the Internet. In its report, the Working Group noted:

"Throughout more than 200 years of history, with periodic amendment, US law has provided the necessary copyright protection for the betterment of our society. The Copyright Act is fundamentally adequate and effective in providing the necessary balance of protection of rights and limitations on those rights to promote the progress of science and the useful arts. Existing copyright law needs only the fine-tuning that technological advances necessitate, in order maintaining the balance of the law in the face of onrushing technology. The Working Group found that most people have trouble understanding the technicalities of intellectual property law and generally do not appreciate the impact that an unauthorized use of a protected work can have on the US economy. In bringing this issue to the public's attention, it would naturally discourage some infringing activity on its own".

By 1994, there was an increase in criminal prosecution under the copyright law. One such case involved David LaMacchia, a 21-year-old student attending the Massachusetts Institute of Technology (MIT). LaMacchia used MIT's computer network system to access the Internet. Using pseudonyms and encryption, LaMacchia set up an electronic bulletin board where he encouraged users to upload software programs and computer games. He then transferred these programs to a second bulletin board where users with secret passwords could download the programs. The worldwide traffic on MIT's computers generated by the free software sent an alert to university officials and federal authorities. LaMacchia was subsequently charged with wire fraud but interestingly not copyright infringement. He entered a motion to dismiss the case, which was granted.

The Court reasoned its decision based on a Supreme Court case, in which the Government's argument that unauthorized use of copyrighted materials was sufficient to render fraud equivalent to wrongful appropriation of statutorily protected rights in copyright. For the court, Justice Blackmun responded that the argument was faulty because "a copyright is comprised of a series of carefully defined and delaminated interests to which the law affords correspondingly exact protections."

The result of the decision exposed a loophole in copyright law where copyright infringers could not be held criminally liable for copyright infringement unless it could be shown that they had somehow profited financially from their infringement. Congress responded in 1997 with the No Electronic Theft Act (NET Act). The NET Act provides copyright owners with a deterrent to protect their rights even when the infringer merely distributes works with no intention of private financial gain.

Congress has stressed that the NET Act is aimed at people who have acted intentionally. Congress included a provision, which emphasized that evidence of reproduction or distribution of a copyrighted work, by itself would not be sufficient to establish willful infringement. The first conviction under the NET Act was in August 1999, when Jeffrey G. Levy, a 22 year old student at the University of Oregon, pled guilty to violating the Net Act by storing pirated software on the university's network, which were later downloaded by the public for free. Levy received 2 years' probation and limited access to the Internet for academic purposes.

Congress also passed the Digital Millennium Copyright Act, (The DMCA). This made on-line providers liable for copyright infringement concerning storage and transmission of materials through their networks. The DMCA called for "actual knowledge" of infringement and was applicable only if the violator profited from his actions. The DMCA was enacted to work with the WIPO treaties and prohibits the circumvention of technological measures, such as passwords or encryption, and devices or services that circumvent such technological measures. The DMCA provides both civil and criminal remedies for violations of these provisions. Thus, if an infringer bypasses some form of encryption to obtain access to a copyrighted software file, he will be in violation of federal copyright law. The anti-circumvention provisions become effective October 28, 2000 (Clark, 2002).

The DMCA provides that "a technological measure protects the rights of a copyright owner," thus, 1201(a) is designed to protect access to a copyright work, while 1201(b) protects the traditional copyrights of the owner. The DMCA exempts certain activities by way of the fair use doctrine. It exempts nonprofit libraries, archives, and educational institutions from criminal penalties and possibly civil remedies if such institutions can demonstrate that they were using the work in good faith for fair use and not for any other purpose. The DMCA also exempts activities that include reverse engineering, encryption research, privacy protection measures, and security testing. Finally, the DMCA provides a "savings clause," which states that it does not affect the rights, remedies, limitations, or defenses to copyright infringement, including fair use.

While the Internet commerce poses risks of infringement, history has provided evidence that this will not bring the author's work, publishing world and copyright registration to an end. After all, society has lived with infringement of that kind since the first publication of the written word. For years, people have been able to copy articles and journals off library shelves or have borrowed books from friends and made copies of selected chapters for themselves or distributed them to others. All of this is considered by the public to be somehow acceptable; perhaps a nonchalant feeling that the author and publisher already have been paid enough and should not be further enriched, at least not at the borrower's expense.

Admittedly, copying in the digital age is faster, cheaper, and better than copying in days gone by and the technology for illicit copying is more widely distributed. This is where understanding how technology itself can be utilized to protect the copyright owner and relying on government and or courts for copyright protection for the successful Internet commerce are needed.

So what does this mean for authors who wish for as much copyright protection as possible? Should they begin with the Copyright Act and utilize its protections by registration. The easier and faster it is to register, the more likely an author will make the effort to copyright his works and protect his rights. The copyright office in Washington is working with Defense Advanced Research Projects Agency (DARPA), the originator of Internet, to develop a system that will make it possible to register materials, to record copyright transfers, and to license on-line. By registering on-line, it will reduce the current wait of months for final processing to days. Currently, on-line registration is available for unpublished technical reports that were registered in conjunction with specific universities.

For the works published on-line, the technology itself can be utilized to institute protection. One protective measure that an author can initiate immediately upon publication on-line is requiring viewers to pay fees to the author and internet service provider before allowing access to on-line publications, mandating the use of a password whereby users agree to certain terms and conditions before access, and including notices to remind users that further reproduction and transmission of the work is unauthorized and constitutes infringement. One such example follows:

Access to and use of this Web site is subject to the following terms and conditions. One may browse for information and entertainment but may not modify, transmit, or revise without the owner's written permission. Communication posted will be treated as unconfidential. Posting or transmitting is unlawful or defamatory material. One use constitutes acceptance of these terms.

For an author's work and or articles for example, published on-line, articles previously published in periodicals have not been infringed by authors' copyrights because the license granted has been exceeded or breached. A 1999 decision by the Second Circuit has held that the Copyright Act gave authors protection in licenses of individual works and can prevent publishers from taking that same license and including the articles in electronic databases (Clark, 2002).

Six freelance writers who were suing their publishers brought the action. The articles had previously been published in periodicals and were later being published on electronic databases, which were available to the public. The court analyzed Section 201(c) of the Act and found that a privilege granted to a collective-work author to use individually copyrighted contributions was limited to the reproduction and distribution of the individual contribution as part of (i) "that particular collective work" which was held to mean a specific edition or issue of a periodical, (ii) "any revision of that collective work" which was held to mean only later or final editions of a particular edition or a specific periodical, and (iii) "any later collective work in the same series" such as a new edition of a dictionary or encyclopedia.

What does this mean for the author? The author must be very specific and detailed about what the license will or will not cover. When registering with the Copyright Office, the author should phrase the license to include the following: "this is an exclusive license to reproduce the work and distribute it by all means and media now known or hereafter discovered, including, without limitation, print, microfilm, and electronic media, as well as the right to display and transmit the work publicly on-line." Any subsequent rights transferred to the publisher should be detailed in that agreement accordingly.

C. Phase Three: Theory Construction

eCommerce is evolving as a means of doing business and shows every sign of continuing to expand at a rapid rate. The rise of this new medium is attracting increasing attention in policy circles. Nevertheless, a lack of adequate data on the magnitude and relevance of electronic supply has made policy-making decisions all the more difficult. eCommerce can be divided into three stages: first, the pre-purchase stage including advertising and information seeking; second, the purchase stage, including purchase and payment; and third, the delivery stage. In principle, all types of products can be advertised and purchased over electronic networks. The potential for electronic delivery is growing rapidly. The final product is presented as digitalized information and transmitted electronically, typically over the Internet. Many services can be supplied as digitalized information, including financial transactions or legal advice. Some information and entertainment products typically characterized as goods, such as books, software, music and videos embody digitalized information that can also be supplied electronically over the Internet. Although all three aspects or stages of electronic commerce defined may have certain trade policy implications, the focus is primarily upon the electronic supply of final products, or in other words, on the third stage (WTO, 2001).

eCommerce already plays an important part in economic activity and its relevance will continue to grow. Although electronic provision will primarily affect service sectors, it will also play an important role in certain manufacturing sectors such as the pharmaceutical, telecom and clothing industries. Most probably, e-commerce will entail productivity gains and price reductions in these sectors. As far as the delivery of products is concerned, the impact of electronic commerce will fall mainly on trade in services rather than trade in goods. In the short term, this trend is likely to continue until electronic trade in these products takes off. As access to Internet becomes more available world-wide and band-with of phone lines expand, the cheaper prices of these products offered through the Web will cause a substitution effect between the physical and electronic trade of digitizable media products. The extent of this will depend on their eventual degree of substitutability (Esteve, Schuknecht, 1999).

Since the early eighteenth century, copyright law has provided the primary regulatory context within which the publishing industry for example has operated. Digital storage media, the Internet in general, and the World Wide Web in particular, have challenged conventional practices and the legal framework. Perhaps the problems posed by technology may be addressed by creating and deploying more technology or by adapting the technology that gave rise to the challenges in the first place.

If protections cannot be successfully devised, implemented, and deployed, longstanding business models in the Internet industry are under serious threat. And to the extent that technological protections are successful, risks arise to the interests of other parties in relation to access to copyrights. In the most basic sense, a business model is the method of doing business by which a company can sustain itself-that is, generate revenue. The business model spells-out how a company makes money by specifying where it is positioned in the value chain. Some models are quite simple. A company produces a good or service and sells it to customers. If all goes well, the revenues from sales exceed the cost of operation and the company realizes a profit. Other models can be more intricately woven. Radio and television broadcasting is a good example. With all the talk about "free" business models on the Web, it is easy to forget that radio, and later television, programming has been broadcast over the airwaves free to anyone with a receiver for much of the past century. The broadcaster is part of a complex network of distributors, content creators, advertisers (and their agencies), and listeners, or viewers. Who makes money and how much is not always clear at the outset. The bottom line depends on many competing factors (Rappa, 2001).

Property is a fundamental part of all cultures. The general rule seems to be that if a resource is scarce or requires labor to create or convert it into a useful state, and then humans will attach property rights to it. Richard Pipes, the eminent Russian scholar and author of *Property and Freedom*, notes that discussions of property since the time of Plato have involved four themes: morality, economics, politics and psychology (DeLong, 2002): First, the general concept of morality is that ownership is derived from labor because each person has the right to the fruits of his industry. There seems to be a strong argument that the creativity that goes into an intellectual product does indeed create a title, not simply for the particular paper and ink with which one expresses an idea, but for the idea.

The second line of justification for property involves the utilitarian or incentive (economic) argument. People work hardest and produce the most when they produce for themselves because money matters. This is as true for artistic expression as it is for shoemakers.   Industrial Revolution was caused by societies' developing ways to protect interests in innovation —not just property rights but contract rights—so as to provide ways to make innovation pay and to create incentives. Property is necessary to produce investment. Who would forgo his current consumption unless he got some future benefit? That leads to the third theme, the political. Property diffuses power and rewards efficient administration. Ownership is a way of decentralizing decisions rather than depending on planning authorities. If resources are not owned, they will be allocated inefficiently not only   in an economic sense but also politically. Property ownership is also an important component of a democratic republic. People do need a stake in society to ensure that its politics do not run off the rails. Pipe's last theme is psychology. He says that property enhances people's sense of identity and self-esteem. Property enhances not just the sense but also the reality of personal autonomy and power, an important function of any social order.

Whether based on natural rights or on utilitarian concepts, Pipe's arguments are deeply conservative in the sense that they have evolved over several millennia in the context of many different societies. Identifying the basic justification for property does not answer all the questions, even in the context of tangible property. There are questions of public facilities, technology, and infrastructure. And there are commons problems spillovers and externalities, and issues of technological change. For example, tangible property is regularly redefined because of technological change. A prime example is the old doctrine that if one owns a property on a waterfront, one can build a pier. But if technological change makes it possible to build a square mile's worth of structures on pilings, suddenly rights change. People used to own their property from the center of the earth to the top of the sky. Then the airplane was invented. Property rights are subject to some reasonable limits, and to revision as technology changes.

The same revision in the light of technological change should and will occur with respect to intellectual property rights. For example, many current copyright issues involve fair use; the doctrine that one can make limited copies without paying or permission. That doctrine arose largely because of transaction costs. If the digital revolution reduces transaction costs so that permission may be obtained and copies made cheaply, then the need for the doctrine may shrink.

One problem with the transaction cost approach is limited access to any current system for micro-payments, necessary if providers of intellectual property are to make available their wares at prices that seem fair to the users. For example, there are songs made available for 25 cents a track. But the most important point is that technological change does not eliminate the need to recognize the claims of intellectual property, and it is not difficult to see why intellectual property should be regarded as fundamentally different from physical property.

Intellectual property protection is frequently viewed in terms of two forces-law and technology. The law articulates what may legally be done, while technology provides some degree of on-the-spot enforcement. In the early days of the software market, for example, distributing floppy disks that had been written in a nonstandard way, making them difficult to copy, enforced the copyright on some programs.

But law and technology are not the only tools available for grappling with the sometimes-difficult task of distributing intellectual property without losing control of it. In the commercial setting, another powerful factor in the mix is the business model. By selecting appropriately from the wide range of business models available, a rights holder may be able to influence significantly the pressure for and degree of illegal copying or other unauthorized uses. By thinking creatively about the nature of the product and the needs of the customer, rights holders may be able to create new business models that are largely unaffected by the properties of digital information (e.g., the ease of replication and distribution) that are problematic in the traditional model of selling content. They may even be able to find business models that capitalize on those very properties. Hence, in addition to its traditional role of specifying the nature of the commercial enterprise, the business model may also play a role in coping with the IP difficulties that arise with products in digital form.

Technological Protection Measures, Online Business Models and DMCA

a. Technical Protection:

The evolution of technology is challenging the status quo of IP management in many ways. This section focused on technical protection services that may be able to assist in controlling the distribution of digital intellectual property on the Internet. The focus here is on how technical tools can assist in meeting the objectives stated throughout the report, as well as what they cannot do and what must therefore be sought elsewhere. Furthermore, this section explores how the tools work, details what each kind of tool brings to bear on the challenges described throughout the report, and projects the expected development and deployment for each tool. For ease of exposition, the presentation in this chapter is framed in terms of protecting individual objects (texts, music albums, movies, and so on); however, many of the issues raised are applicable to collections (e.g., libraries and databases), and many of the techniques discussed are relevant to them as well (NAP, 2000): A number of general points are important about technical protection:

- Technology provides means, not ends; it can assist in enforcing IP policy, but it cannot provide answers to social, legal, and economic questions about the ownership of and rights over works, nor can it make up for incompletely or badly answered questions.

- No technical protection can protect perfectly. Technology changes rapidly, making previously secure systems progressively less secure. Social environments also change, with the defeat of security systems attracting more (or less) interest in the population. Just as in physical security systems, there are inherent trade-offs between the engineering design and implementation quality of a system on the one hand and the cost of building and deploying it on the other. The best that can be hoped for is steady improvement in technical protection quality and affordability and keeping a step ahead of those bent on defeating the systems.

- While technical protection for intellectual property copyright is often construed as protecting the rights of rights holders to collect revenue, this viewpoint is too narrow. Technical protection offers additional important services, including verifying the authenticity of information (i.e., indicating whether it comes from the source claimed and whether it has been altered-either inadvertently or fraudulently). Information consumers will find this capability useful for obvious reasons. Publishers as well need authenticity controls to protect their brand quality.

- As with any security system, the quality and cost of a technical protection should be tailored to the values of and risks to the resources it helps protect.

- Again, as with any security system, there are different degrees of protection. Some technical protection is designed to keep honest people honest and provide only a modest level of enforcement; more ambitious uses seek to provide robust security against professional pirates.

- As with any software, technical protection is subject to design and implementation errors that need to be uncovered by careful research and investigation. Professional cryptologists and digital security experts look for flaws in existing services in order to define better products.

- Technical protection almost invariably causes some inconvenience to their users. Part of the ongoing design effort is to eliminate such inconvenience or at least to reduce it to tolerable levels.

- The amount of inconvenience caused by a technical protection has been correlated historically with its degree of protection. As a result, in the commercial context, overly stringent protection is as bad as inadequate protection: In either extreme--no protection or complete protection (i.e., making content inaccessible)--revenues are zero. Revenues climb with movement away from the extremes; the difficult empirical task is finding the right balance.

- Protective technologies that are useful within special-purpose devices (e.g., cable-television set-top boxes or portable digital music players) are quite different from those intended for use in general-purpose computers. For network-attached general-purpose computers, software alone cannot achieve the level of technical protection attainable with special-purpose hardware. However, software-only measures will doubtless be in wide use soon.

The following are the most important technical protection mechanisms, suggesting how each can be fit into an overall protection scheme, describing the limitations of each, and sketching current research directions. There are several classes of mechanisms (NAP, 2000):

- *Security and integrity features of computer operating systems* include, for example, the traditional file access privileges enforced by the system.

- *Rights management languages* express in machine-readable form the rights and responsibilities of owners, distributors, and users, enabling the computer to determine whether requested actions fall within a permitted range. These languages can be viewed as an elaboration of the languages used to express file access privileges in operating systems.

- *Encryption* allows digital works to be scrambled so that only legitimate users can unscramble them.

- *Persistent encryption* allows the consumer to use information while the system maintains it in an encrypted form.

- *Watermarking* embeds information (e.g., about ownership) into a digital work in much the same way that paper can carry a watermark. A digital watermark can help owners track copying and distribution of digital works.

For effective protection, the developer of an IP-delivery service must choose the right ingredients and attempt to weave them together into an end-to-end technical protection system. The term "end-to-end" emphasizes the maintenance of control over the content at all times; the term "protection system" emphasizes the need to combine various services so that they work together as seamlessly as possible.

Protecting intellectual property is a variant of computing and communications security, an area of study that has long been pursued both in research laboratories and for real-world application. Security is currently enjoying renewed emphasis because of its relevance to conducting business online, eBusiness.

b. The Impact of the Digital Environment on Business Models

This section explores a variety of models and their impact on the need for technical protection mechanisms and considers the interaction of law, technology, and business models.

As noted in Chapter 1, the introduction of digital media changes the business environment in a number of important ways. The focus here is on the impact of digital media on the intellectual property issues involved in the commercial distribution of content.

Most business models for traditional copyrighted works involve the sale of a physical item that becomes the property of the customer. The economics of the transaction include the costs associated with creating the initial content and first copy of the work (first-copy costs), the costs of reproduction, marketing, distribution, and other overhead costs. Although copyright does not protect subsequent redistribution of the physical copy, in many cases further reproduction and distribution are protected de facto by the costs associated with creating or re-creating a physical copy nearly equal in quality to the original (NAP, 2000).

Digital information is not of course the first technology to challenge this business model. Photocopying permits the reproduction and distribution of protected works, and although the quality may not be equal to the original, if made available at a low enough price some customers will find photocopies to be acceptable substitutes. Videotapes and audiotapes are similarly vulnerable.

Digital media disrupt the traditional business model by drastically lowering the cost and effort of reproduction and distribution and by producing copies indistinguishable from the original. While rights holders and consumers benefit from this, so may infringers. Additional impacts of the digital medium include the ability to reproduce material in private, increasing the difficulty of detection and the ability to copy and distribute material very quickly, often before an intellectual property owner can even detect the offense, let alone seek injunctive relief. Natural barriers to infringement are thus eroded in the digital environment. This erosion may be sufficiently extreme at times that rights holders may be wise to reevaluate their fundamental business model. In some cases digital information may be simply unprotectable, at least in practice if not in law and in principle.

Digital media have other impacts on business models as well. Licensing, rather than the sale is becoming increasingly popular for digital media, in part because of the difficulty of retaining control after a sale. In this model the customer becomes a user rather than an owner, buying access to a service rather than a physical good. This raises important issues: in a world of distribution by paper, the customer owns a physical copy of the work. What is "owned" in a service offered over a network? If a library discontinues a subscription to an online journal, for example, what rights, if any, does it have to the intellectual property it had been accessing? While networked services are far from new-Dialog and Lexis-Nexis are now more than 20 years old-the nature of access rights has become a major concern with information products and must be factored into the business model.

Those distributing intellectual property in digital form over networks find they are in a business environment changed by customer perceptions and expectations. The perception is that distribution costs are lower, so customer expectations are that prices will be lower than for analog equivalents. In some cases this is true, as with, for example, the replacement of printed software manuals with online or ondisk help. Here the economics clearly favor digital formats over paper. In many other cases, however, first-copy costs are higher with digital products, partly because consumers have come to expect more from digital information (e.g., indexing, searching, hyperlinks, multimedia). There are, in addition, new costs associated with digital distribution that offset at least some of the decreased traditional manufacturing costs (e.g., the cost of keeping up with the rapid evolution in browser capabilities and in Web languages).

This pressure for low-priced goods is exacerbated by the fact that on the Web, by far the largest single supply of digital information, free information currently predominates, creating expectations that content will be available free or for low prices. There is also the misperception that "free" equates to "public domain," leading some to believe that if it can be downloaded freely, it is unprotected by intellectual property law. Traditional business models are thus stressed in a number of ways by digital information; of particular significance here is the erosion of natural barriers to infringement and the pressure for inexpensive goods.

Business Models for Handling Information

Traditional business models include a wide variety of possibilities, including goods paid for solely by the buyer, goods totally or partially subsidized by advertisers, and goods given away at no charge, as well as mixes of these models. These are reviewed briefly here to indicate how they are used in the digital environment and to set the stage for exploring less traditional business models in the next section (NAP, 2000):

Traditional Business Models

Some traditional business models are outlined below:

1. Business models based on fees for products or services

- *Single transaction purchase.* Examples: Videos, books, some software, music CDs, some text CD-ROMs, and article photocopies (document delivery).
- *Subscription purchase.* Examples: Newsletter and most journal subscriptions.
- *Single-transaction license.* Examples: Some software and most text CD-ROMs.

- *Serial-transaction license* (usually where there is a flat fee for unlimited use). Example: Electronic subscription to a single title (this is different from item 1c above in that the license will often be renewed from year to year upon payment of fees).

- *Site licenses* (these are generally also flat fees for unlimited use, but with a broader licensed community). Examples: Software licenses for whole companies, a package containing all electronic journals from a publisher for all members of a university community.

- *Payment per electronic use*. Examples: Information resources paid for per search, per time online, or per article accessed.

2. Business models relying on advertising

- *Combined subscription and advertising*. Examples: Newspapers, consumer and business-to-business magazines, Web sites such as the *Wall Street Journal*, and America Online.

- *Advertising income only*. Examples: Many Web sites and controlled circulation magazines.

3. "Free" distribution business models

- *Free distribution* (no hidden motive). Examples: Scholarly papers on preprint servers and software like Apache, available for free.

- *Free samples*--the traditional notion of providing an introduction to the product. Example: A demonstration version of a software package in the expectation that the customer will want a full or more up-to-date version.

- *Information goods for those who buy something else or have another income-producing relationship with the information provider*. Example: Free browser software offered to increase traffic on an income-producing Web site.

- *Government information or other information in the public domain*. Examples: Standards, economic data, statutes, and regulations.

- *Prestige/vanity/some start-ups*. Example: Garage band wanting to get publicity for other services.

Less Traditional Business Models

A variety of other business models have been explored in an attempt to confront the IP difficulties encountered in the digital world. Some of these are derived from models used for traditional products, while others appear to be unique to the world of information products. Eight of these less traditional business models are described below (NAP, 2000):

1. *Give away the information product and earn revenue from an auxiliary product or service*. Examples of auxiliary products: Free access to an online newspaper in exchange for basic demographic data; the revenue-generating auxiliary product is the database of information about readers. Free distribution of (some) music because it enhances the market for auxiliary goods and services associated with the artist (attendance at concerts, T-shirts, posters, etc.). Example of auxiliary service: The Linux operating system is distributed for free; the market is in service-support, training, consulting, and customization.

2. *Give away the initial information product and sell upgrades*. Example: Antivirus software, where the current version is often freely downloadable; the revenue-generating product is the subsequent updates (along with support service).

3. *Extreme customization*--Make the product so personal that few people other than the purchaser would want it. Examples: Search engine output, personalized newspapers, and personalized CDs. MusicMaker will create a CD containing the tracks exactly in the sequence specified by a customer.

4. *Provide a large product in small piece, making it easy to browse but difficult to get in its entirety.* Examples: Online encyclopedias, databases, and many Web sites.

5. *Give away digital content because it complements (and increases demand for) the traditional product.* Examples: The MIT Press makes the full text of some books and reports available online; this has apparently increased sales of the hard-copy versions.

6. *Give away one piece of digital content because it creates a market for another.* Examples: The Netscape browser was freely distributed in part to increase demand for their server software; Adobe's Acrobat Reader is freely distributed to increase demand for the Acrobat document preparation software.

7. *Allow free distribution of the product but request payment* (perhaps offering additional value in the paid-for version). Example: Shareware. Where shareware versions have time-limited functionality or are incomplete demonstration versions, this is quite similar to the "free sample" model above.

8. *Position the product for low-priced, mass market distribution.* Examples: Microsoft Windows ('95 and '98).

These examples illustrate that far more than immediate production costs enter into pricing decisions. They also demonstrate the trend of relating pricing and other decisions to efforts to develop relationships with customers.

The Controversial DMCA

The Digital Millennium Copyright Act (DMCA) did not solve IP copyright issues. Although many of the legal controversies that have swirled since its October 1998 passage trace their roots to other elements of copyright law, the DMCA created a new feature in copyright law that has crystallized why so many technology entrepreneurs, academics, and computer users object to what they regard the overreaching nature of copyright-law (Clark, 2002).

This single feature is the ban on individuals cracking encryption codes used by content owners to restrict access to digital works on which they hold copyrights. In the encoded Section 1201 of the Copyright Act, the statue reads: "No person shall circumvent a technological measure that effectively controls access to a work protected under this title" (17 U>S.C. 1201(a)(1)(A)). The definitions of those terms are broad enough to bar almost all unauthorized decryption of content. Subsequent language in the section also prohibits the manufacture, release, or sale of products, services, and devices that can crack encryption designed to thwart either access to or copying of material unauthorized by the copyright holder. For the first time in history, it is not the copyright violation that was the crime. The creation of the technological tools to violate copyright became the crime. The law germinated from a 1995 "white paper" drafter by Bruce Lehman, the first patent office chief and intellectual property expert in the Clinton administration. Heavily supported by copyright holders, the key rationale behind the white paper was that content owners would be unwilling to put their content in digital form were it not for new laws against those who defeat the digital locks they place on their products. The anti-circumvention concept gained momentum in 1996 when it was endorsed in a WIPO Copyright Treaty. It was subsequently adopted as DMCA's Title 1, the WIPO Copyright and Performance and Phonograms Treaties Implementation Act.

The current copyright law points to many expansions in its power over the past decade. Among the more recent measures are the Digital Performance Right in Sound Recording Act of 1995 (creating a new copyright in digital music performances), the No Electronic Theft Act of 1997 (eliminating non-commercial use as a defense against copyright infringement), the Sony Bono Copyright Term Extension Act of 1998 (adding 20 years to the already-lengthy terms of all copyrights), portions of DMCA mandating new royalties for digital music performances, and the Digital Theft Deterrence and Copyright Damages Improvement Act of 1999 (penalties for infringement). There are a few measures that arguably limit the power of copyright holders, including the Fairness in Music Licensing Act of 1998 (granting a limited exemption from music licensing for food service and drinking establishments), and elements of DMCA that limited Internet service provider liability for copyright infringement if they comply with procedures to take down allegedly infringing material from Web sites they control (Clark, 2002).

Some of those changes in law are directly at issue in current copyright controversies, such as the debate over extending copyright terms-a challenge to Congress' authority over copyright law that has been accepted by the Supreme Court and what rates should be paid by Internet radio stations for the right to stream digital ecommerce transactions over the Web. Other issues, like what to do about the free digital music Web site Napster, which filed for bankruptcy in June 2002, and its many successor clones, delve into more fundamental questions: how file-sharing technologies can be held liable for contributing to the copyright infringement of their users, and whether users of a technology have a "fair use" defense against charges of infringement.

Yet it is the DMCA's anti-circumvention prohibition, which has been upheld by the Second Circuit Court of Appeals that is likely to have more sweeping effects on the future of copyright law and eCommerce transactions because it is seen as under-girding the technological protection measures increasingly taken by content owners. This provision is also an illuminating lens through which to view the copyright debate.

Although the DMCA's section 1201 has been at issue in an extremely limited number of court cases thus far, its implications for the future are enormous because of the desire by copyright holders to deploy more sophisticated copyright protection devices. The movie, book, and commercial software industries already routinely use such digital locks in an effort to stymie unauthorized users from accessing and copying portions of works for which they have paid.

An example of such technology is the Content Scrambling System (CSS) for digital videodisks (DVDs) developed by a group of technology companies working in collaboration with the motion picture industry through the Copy Protection Technical Working Group (CPTWG). The technology, which is governed by the DVD-Copy Control Association controlled by both Hollywood and the consumer electronics manufacturers, scrambles the content on the DVDs in a manner that makes them unviewable unless they are played on a DVD-licensed player. Those players, in turn, deactivate all copyright functions (Clark, 2002):

But after Norwegian teenager Jon Johansen cracked the encryption code and published it on the Internet as DeCSS, Web sites including the hacker magazine 2600 posted the software and provided links to other sites that had posted it as well. At Universal Studios V. Reimerdes, the major Hollywood studios sued 2600 Web Site owners Eric Reimerders, Eric Corley, and Roman Kazan, none of whom were themselves accused of using the software code to engage in video piracy or commit other copyright violations. Purely on grounds of violating the DMCA, the company won in both district court and before the Second Circuit Court of Appeals. The Electronic Frontier Foundation (EFF), a civil liberties group representing the defendants and taking the lead on litigation opposing the DMCA, has sought reconsideration of the decision by the full court of appeals.

A second case involved Princeton University computer science professor Edward Felten, who found holes in the Secure Digital Music Initiative, a copyright protection scheme supported by the Recording Industry Association of America (RIAA). Attorneys for RIAA and Verance, one of the companies involved in designing elements of the music encryption, threatened Felton with a lawsuit alleging DMCA violations if he presented his research at an academic conference in April 2001. Felten backed down, but the media outcry against the RIAA led it to say that it never intended to block Felten from speaking, and he did so at an August 2001 computer conference. EFF sought an injunction against it, but a federal district judge in New Jersey threw out the case on the grounds that there was no case or controversy at issue.

A third case was the criminal prosecution of Dmitry Sklyyarove, a Russian programmer arrested and charged in July 2001 after he attended a prominent hacker conference in Las Vegas. In the first criminal application of the law, the U.S. Attorney's Office in San Francisco alleged that Sklyarove and Elcomsoft, his Russian employer, had reverse-engineered Adobe's e-Book reader, permitting users to decrypt electronic books and read them "in the clear". Adobe's product is an example of the emerging field of digital rights management technologies. It relies upon encryption to forbid such reading, because without the scrambling, computer users could email e-books to their friends or share them with strangers over a peer-to-peer network (P2P) like Napster--where the material is transferred from one personal computer to another over the Internet. But the Elcomsoft work-around also permitted a user to read an e-book on both his desktop and his laptop, an application that some regard as a fair use defense under copyright law. Prosecutors initiated their charges after being informed of Elcomsoft's activities in a meeting with Adobe executives. Again after public outcry-and meeting with Eff officials–Adobe said it did not support his prosecution. In December 2001, the U.S. Attorney's office deferred the charges against Sklyarov–essentially dropping them–although the office insists it is continuing to build a case against Elcomsoft for future trail.

The new threats of DMCA actions are on the horizon. Because the recording industry fears declining sales of CDs because of the widespread availability of digital music files on P2P networks like Aimster, Grokster, Kazaa, and Morpheus–each of which they have sued– studios have began introducing CDs that will not play on computers at all. A digital flaw inserted onto the CDs in the manufacturing process renders them inaudible except on conventional, dedicated CD players. Done in an effort to stop consumers from copying and sharing digital files ripped into MP3 tracks, the effort again runs afoul of consumers expectations that they are able to make personal and backup copies of their CDs, including the ability to mix and rearrange tracks before burning them onto their own CDs, or put them on a portable MP3 player. Technology providers have said that they can provide the tools to enable consumers to play such copy-protected CDs on their computers, but have held back from doing so because of the DMCA's strict language (Clark, 2002).

Codified in the Copyright Act at 17 U.S.C 107, fair use provides judges with four factors that they must consider in determining whether a copyright infringement has occurred: 1) the purpose and character of the use, including whether it is commercial or for non-profit educational purposes; 2) the nature of the copyrighted work itself; 3) whether the section used constitutes a substantial portion of the work as a whole; and 4) the effect of the use upon the potential market for and value of the copyrighted work.

The question about circumvention to permit fair use raises one of the core questions about the DMCA: what happens to individuals traditional conception of fair use when companies use digital rights management technologies to lock down copyrighted material? And should a copyright owner be able to rely on the law to limit the use of their copyrighted material when their technologies fail? The examples above show that the sweeping nature of DMCA could easily lead courts to privilege copyrights over other rights–including the right to free speech in the development of software code (Clark, 2002).

And yet the questions above are given especially sharp focus by the introduction of legislation that goes considerably beyond this. Hollywood studios have persuaded Senate Commerce Chairman Ernest Fritz Hollings to introduce legislation that would actually bar the creation of all computer software and hardware that does not include a government-sanctioned digital rights management (DRM) technology. Dubbed the Consumer Broadband and Digital Television Promotion Act and presented as a measure designed to spur their adoption, S. 2048 was introduced in March 2002.

S.2048 is an extreme example of legislative deference to perceived interest of some copyright holders at the expense of nearly everyone else. It gives the information technology industry and Hollywood one year to create security system standards that will provide effective security for copyrighted works. If they agree, the Federal Communications Commission will implement them; if they do not, the FCC is obliged to attempt to create its own standards for digital rights management. Device manufacturers and software creators who fail to include the mandated standard would be subject to the same criminal penalties as are violators of the DMCA.

In other words, beyond simply criminalizing the circumvention of private digital rights management technologies voluntarily deployed by copyright holders, the Holling legislation would itself mandate the DRM technology to be used, force compliance upon the entire technology industry, and then penalize those who failed to use it as if they had cracked them.

VI. Chapter Summary

The value of IP assets relative to physical assets has increased because of the importance of technology and creative works in the modern economy. IP is often traded (or licensed) in its own right without trading in the value of an underlying product or service by means of patent or other IP licenses from a rights owner to another.

This chapter provided the description of qualitative research methodology based on content analysis procedures used for testing research hypothesis, exploring research questions, and building theory. This chapter concludes that there are several reasons why IP is important to eCommerce and eCommerce is important to IP. eCommerce, more than other business systems, often involves selling products and services that are based on IP and its licensing. Software, music, pictures, photos, designs, training modules, and systems can all be traded through eCommerce wherein, IP is the main component of value in the transaction. IP is important because the things of value that are traded on the Internet must be protected using technological security systems and IP laws, lest they be stolen or pirated and whole businesses destroyed.

Also, IP is involved in making eCommerce work. The systems that allow the Internet to function-software, networks, designs, chips, routers and switches, the user interface, and so on-are forms of IP and often protected by IP rights. eCommerce businesses and Internet related businesses are based on product or patent licensing; because so many different technologies are required to create a product, companies often outsource the development of some component of products or share technologies through licensing arrangements. If every company had to develop and produce all technological aspects of every product independently, development of high technology products would be impossible. The economics of eCommerce depends on companies working together to share, through licensing, the opportunities and risks of business.

eCommerce based businesses usually hold a great deal of their value in IP; so the valuation of E-Commerce business will be affected by whether a business is protected IP or not (WIPO). One of the most remarkable characteristics of eCommerce is that it occurs globally. IP may be used and licensed in many countries simultaneously. The global characteristic of eCommerce businesses affects IP in a number of ways. It makes it difficult to find the infringer and enforce IP rights that are violated on the Internet. It is unclear what courts will have jurisdiction over disputes relating to eCommerce and IP. Also, laws affecting IP vary from country to country so levels of protection may be different.

Intellectual property is typically conceived of first and foremost as a legal construct. Although law may constrain what one may (legally) do, equally powerful constraints arise from forces such as markets, social norms, and the values embedded in hardware and software (Lessig,1999). Markets put things within or out of economic reach, social norms urge conformity with group values, and hardware and software encourage some behaviors and make others impossible.

The various forces differ in the explicitness of the values underlying them. Although laws generally result from a process that in principle is public and encourages examination of values and motivations, the same cannot be said of technology. The software written to control access to a Web site is a form of private regulation, and the process that created it rarely involves explicit discussion of the values embedded in and enforced by the program.

Technical protection services (i.e., hardware and software used to protect IP) may offer content producers and distributors the important ability to manage access to their intellectual property, but those mechanisms may also enforce restrictions on the use of content that do not align with the (limited) rights of authors specified in copyright law. That law explicitly embraces certain public policy goals, but technical protection mechanisms and the policies they enforce may reflect a choice to overlook or to ignore those goals, with little or no opportunity for the public discussion or evaluation that goes into the creation of statutes.

The more general phenomenon here is the potential for substituting one force for another, and the consequences this may have for the degree of public participation in shaping society. To the extent that software is substituted for statute, for example, a form of privately created regulation is being used rather than publicly adopted laws. Such substitution should not be accepted by default or permitted to go unexamined as discussed in the next chapter, Analysis and Results.

Chapter 4: Analysis And Results

I. Introduction

In the last five years, there has been a rise in the exploration of many technical mechanisms intended to protect intellectual property in digital form, along with attempts to develop commercial products and services based on those mechanisms. This chapter analyzes the IP protection technology data, explains the technology's capabilities and limitations, and explores the consequences these capabilities may have for the distribution of and access to IP copyright.   This chapter also analyzes the role of business models in protecting IP copyright. Protection is typically conceived of in legal and technical terms, determined by what the law permits and what technology can enforce. Business models add a third, powerful element to the mix, one that can serve as an effective means of making more digital content available in new ways and that can be an effective deterrent to illegitimate uses of IP.

This study examines four major positions (mandatory DRM, DMCA, Fair Use, and Free Speech) about how extensive copyright law should be and evaluated the justification for each position for digital transactions. This study also discusses the survey results and challenges to Section 1201. Finally, it suggests that by injecting anti-circumvention into the concept of copyright law, the DMCA exposes inherent weaknesses in what copyright law should be.

II. Analysis and Results

The analysis and evaluation of the results include technological protection measures, online business models, four major positions (mandatory DRM, fair use, DMCA and free speech), and surveys for IP copyright laws and regulations.

A. Technological protections/Measures

Cryptography is a crucial enabling technology for IP management. The goal of encryption is to scramble objects so that they are not understandable or usable until they are unscrambled. The technical terms for scrambling and unscrambling are "encrypting" and "decrypting." Encryption facilitates IP management by protecting content against disclosure or modification both during transmission and while it is stored. If content is encrypted effectively, copying the files is nearly useless because there is no access to the content without the decryption key. Software available off the shelf provides encryption that is for all practical purposes unbreakable, although much of the encrypting software in use today is somewhat less robust (NAP, 2000).

Many commercial IP management strategies plan a central role for what is called "symmetric-key" encryption, so called because the same key is used both to encrypt and decrypt the content. Each object (e.g., movie, song, text, graphic, software application) is encrypted by the distributor with a key unique to that object; the encrypted object can then be widely distributed (e.g., placed on a Web site). The object's key is given only to appropriate recipients (e.g., paying customers), typically via a different, more secure route, perhaps one that relies on special hardware.

Any encryption system must be designed and built very carefully as there are numerous and sometimes very subtle ways in which information can be captured. Among the more obvious is breaking the code; if the encryption is not powerful enough, mathematical techniques may be used to decrypt the message even without the key. If the key-distribution protocol is flawed, an unauthorized person may be able to obtain the key via either high technology (e.g., wiretapping) or "social engineering" (e.g., convincing someone with access to the key to supply it, a widely used approach). If the system used to read the decrypted information is not designed carefully, the decrypted information may be left accessible (e.g., in a temporary file) after it has been displayed to the user. The point to keep in mind is that cryptography is no magic bullet; using it effectively requires both considerable engineering expertise and attention to social and cultural factors (e.g., providing incentives for people to keep messages secret). Whether a technological protection system (TPS) is successful begins with its inherent technical strength but depends ultimately on both the product it protects and the business in which it is deployed. The vendor interested in protecting content is only partly concerned with whether a TPS satisfies an abstract technical definition of security. Indeed, people who are sufficiently motivated and knowledgeable can circumvent most of the techniques discussed in this section. Vendors have more concrete concerns: does the TPS deter enough potential thieves and facilitate enough use by paying customers to produce a profitable content-distribution business? Some of the properties that bring a TPS in line with a business model include:

- *Usability.* A protection system that is cumbersome and difficult to use may deter paying customers. If that happens, it is a failure, no matter how successful it may be at preventing theft.

- *Appropriateness to the content.* The cost of designing, developing, and deploying the protection system has to be in harmony with the market for the content. For content that is inexpensive or already available in a reasonably priced, non-Internet medium, there is no point for an expensive TPS that drives up the price of Internet delivery.

- *Appropriateness to the threat.* Preventing honest customers from giving copies to their friends may require nothing more than a reasonably priced product, a good distribution system, and a clear set of instructions. At the other end of the spectrum, preventing theft of

- extremely valuable content that must at some point reside in a networked PC requires a very sophisticated TPS, and even the best available with current technology may not be good enough.

The cost-benefit analysis needed to design or choose an appropriate TPS-if indeed there is one-is difficult but necessary. Distributors can lose in the marketplace because they choose a TPS that is too sophisticated or too expensive just as easily as they can because they choose one that is too weak.

ii. Business Models

a. Business Models as a Means of Dealing with Intellectual Property

Business model design and selection can play a significant role in grappling with questions of IP protection. The choice of a model has significant consequences for the role that IP rights enforcement will play and, importantly, models are available that require far less enforcement. Hence, one approach to IP rights in a world where digital content is difficult to control entails selecting a business model that does not require strict control (NAP, 2000).

Relying on a business model rather than a technical protection mechanism may also offer some leverage with the difficulty described in Chapter 1. With the emergence of computers and networking into the mainstream of daily life, attempting to enforce IP rights increasingly involves the difficult task of controlling private behavior. Where IP enforcement has historically been an issue between corporations and has historically regulated public acts, the vastly increased means and opportunity for using (and abusing) IP in the hands of individuals have led to increased concern with the private actions of individuals. Where such private actions of individuals are concerned, detection and enforcement are more difficult, making the law a less effective tool. Technical protection mechanisms may help in such circumstances by making illegal or unauthorized actions more difficult, but the selection of an appropriate business model can reduce the motivation for those actions in the first place.

There are, of course, limits to the applicability of these models. Some properties, such as first-run movies, are unlikely ever to be given away, simply because of their high value. In that case other means of dealing with IP issues become more relevant, such as technical protection mechanisms (e.g., as in DVD) or perhaps not making any digital versions of the intellectual property available to consumers.

In formulating a plan for the commercial distribution of intellectual property, then, the rights holder is well advised to consider all three important areas: exploring what boundaries are set by the law, what technical protections are practical and cost-effective, and how the business model will produce revenue. The law sets the foundational context in which the other two must function, drawing the boundaries that specify both what legal protection exists against unauthorized reproduction, distribution, and use, and the limits on the rights holder's monopoly (e.g., provisions for public access or time limitations on the term of protection). Technical protection mechanisms and business models can then play complementary roles in grappling with the difficulties of distributing IP content in digital, each capable of reducing the degree of "leakage" of the product.

All three factors interact. Technology influences the selection of a business model. Any technical protection mechanism has both cost and benefit; it costs the producer to implement and may produce nuisance value for the customer (e.g., nonstandard floppies), but may also pay off in lower rates of illegal copying. IP law also influences business model selection, for example, the limited lifetime of copyright protection must be considered in developing the business model. And, in some cases, the selection of a business model may obviate the need for technical protection.

Selecting a business model for an information product is difficult in part because of the curious economics of information products. This section summarizes a few observations that have consequences in the marketplace and for the selection of a business model.

The duration of economic value varies over an extraordinary range, from a stock market quote (one minute or less) to a classic play (e.g., timeless Greek tragedies), but generally the economic value of most works is far shorter than the standard period of copyright protection. However, while duration of value is often short (sometimes fleeting), changes in value over time can be quite unpredictable. Today's news is valuable; yesterday's nearly worthless, while the news of 100 years ago is valuable again.

Curiously, there is value in both scarce information and in widely disseminated information. Scarcity confers obvious value. Consider the stock tip known by few others. But wide dissemination of information can produce value as well. Consider network effects in software, where the value of a program increases as more people use it, particularly as it approaches the status of a standard.

For digital information products, there are large first-copy costs and almost negligible production and distribution costs. Particularly in the absence of IP protection, this can produce a very sharp decline in product value over time, as it becomes an easily copied commodity.

A few generalizations are available about selecting business models to deal with IP issues. As a general observation, business models in which intellectual property can be widely disseminated at low cost are more successful in addressing intellectual property problems than are businesses that rely on higher prices and a small number of units distributed. The reasons are straightforward: If the cost of reproduction or piracy is high relative to the cost of acquiring the work legitimately, intellectual property problems will be less serious. Examples include newspapers, magazines, and paperback books.

More interesting, perhaps, is finding ways to permit low-cost distribution. The mass communication media have been the most successful because they make use of advertiser support to cover most or all of the cost of production and distribution, a model widely adopted on the Web. The use of rental markets as in videos (and formerly books) works well where such markets are feasible. The use of intellectual property to promote the use of other products (e.g., free browsers to promote Web traffic) is one of the few successful models available of widespread distribution of a digital information product for (very) low cost.

There is reason to approach doing business on the Web or in other electronic forms with some optimism, for there are a variety of business models to consider. As pointed out by Shapiro and Varian (1998), the goal for commercial information creators and owners is to maximize revenues, not protection. Business models will continue to evolve with the maturation of digital products; their careful design and selection may help to create effective ways to do business in the information world.

B. Intellectual Property Implications of Traditional Business Models

Models derive all revenue from fees for the product or service. Here revenues depend on the number of copies sold or licenses signed, making the rights holder more sensitive to illegal copying, piracy, and even fair use, to the degree that any of these replace the purchase of a copy. Success of a business model of this type depends, in part, on the producer's ability to control post sale copying (NAP, 2000).

Specifically, Models 1a (single transaction purchase) and 1b (subscription purchase) are outright purchases, with all of the first-sale and existing copyright implications as to fair use. Models 1c (single transaction license), 1d (serial transaction license), and 1e (site license), as licenses, are attempts to remove any ambiguity in the copyright law by creating an enforceable contract between the rights holder and the user. Such contracts may attempt to impose other desires of the rights holder through the terms in the contract. While nominally clearer, many licenses are frequently ignored, not understood, not known about by the end user, or otherwise fail to satisfy all parties. Model 1f (pay per use) is a fee for service that may be implemented through either sale or licensing models.

Business models that include advertising (Models 2a and 2b) add more balance to the revenue stream. Subscription prices are held down or eliminated because a large number of qualified recipients help to ensure advertising revenues. Intellectual property concerns may be more related to illegal reproduction and framing--for example, it is important to ensure that users come to the rights holders' Web site so that advertisements are viewed by users as intended by the rights holders. There is less concern about unauthorized access when the sole income is from advertising. Many Web sites of this type require user registration as a way to identify viewers to advertisers but, for many others, simply counting page views or some other measure of traffic is sufficient.

In the free distribution business models (Models 3a through 3e), reproduction is generally not an issue: except for the case where use of intellectual property is tied to the purchase of some other product, the information owner is clearly seeking as widespread a dissemination as possible by giving free access. The principal intellectual property concerns here relate to preservation of the integrity of the information, proper citation if someone else uses the information, and the prevention of commercial use of the material by unauthorized users.

C. Intellectual Property Implications of Less Traditional Business Models

The less traditional models all reduce the need for enforcement of intellectual property protection against reproduction. The first two are accompanied by foregoing any attempt to generate revenue from the digital content, using it instead as a means of creating demand for services or physical products, neither of which are subject to the replication difficulties of digital products. Giving away digital content as a complement to a traditional product works because reading information online is still awkward and because most people are not willing to print out a multi-hundred-page book. Selling upgrades relies on the relatively short shelf life of the original product; antivirus software is typically upgraded every 3 months. Extreme customization renders moot any need for enforcing IP protection, because only the original purchaser is interested in the product. Parceling out the product in small pieces simply makes it difficult to copy the entire product, in part restoring a barrier to infringement that comes naturally with physical products (NAP, 2000).

Giving away one digital product to promote another reduces the need for IP enforcement for the product given away, but it does little to reduce the need for IP enforcement for the charged-for product. One related strategy is to differentiate individuals from organizations. For example, Netscape and Adobe give away programs that individuals use in order to sell the (more expensive) programs purchased by organizations. This approach takes advantage of the comparative ease of enforcing IP rights against organizations as compared to detecting and prosecuting infringement by individuals. It also capitalizes on the expectation that organizations may generate use that is valuable enough for them to pay for the product and recognizes that organizations also have processes and resources to comply more easily with IP laws and license agreements.

Free and low-cost mass-market distribution is in the spirit of making the product cheaper to buy than it is to steal. It is worth noting that stealing an information product or service typically comes at a cost. An individual needs to expend the cost, time, and effort to obtain the product or service through infringing means and faces possible downstream costs such as refusal of technical support. When costs (i.e., the price to buy versus the total costs to steal) converge, the need for IP enforcement clearly diminishes.

III. Four Positions

1. Mandatory DRM

Walt Disney Co. and New Corp. executive-Shae been among the loudest advocates of the principles embodied in Hooling S. 2048, and they have gradually dragged along the other five major studios that are members of the Motion Picture Association of America. In testimony before a February 2002 Senate Commerce Committee hearing on Hollings draft legislation, Disney CEO Michael Eisner and News Corp. Chief Operating Officer Peter Chernin argued that because Internet piracy of digital content is so widespread, the technology industry must be forced to create the tools to stop their movies from being transmitted digitally (Clark, 2002).As mentioned above, Hollywood collaborated with technology industry representatives on the creation of the DVD encryption scheme, an effort begun in 1996 in a technical working group. Also emerging from that effort has been a proposal by a consortium of five equipment manufacturers–Intel Copr. Matsushitat Electric Industry Co., Toshiba Corp., Sony Corp., and Hitachi Ltd.–to provide technologies that impede unauthorized access to and copying of cable and satellite broadcasts of digital content. Sony Corp.'s Sony Pictures Entertainment and AOL time Warner's Warner Brothers have signed on to the consortium's technology- dubbed- "5C" because it was first preferred by five consumer electronics manufacturers, although it is now accepted by many others–

others held off because of a desire to protections for over-the-air broadcasts of digital television.

Almost all observers acknowledge that unauthorized copying of cable and satellite systems can be limited by voluntary agreements because of a chain of licensing agreements that require distributors, equipment manufacturers, and consumers themselves to abide by such limitations. But such agreements are unable to provide such content protection when television programs and movies are broadcast over-the-air and in the clear, i.e. without encryption. (To broadcast digital content in an encrypted format would mean that hundreds of millions of analog television sets would be unable to view them.) And television and movie producers perceive danger in making such unencrypted digital broadcasts available because digital copies are easily reproduced and do not degrade. For them, the only alternative is simply not broadcasting digitally.

That problem could be solved by means of a broadcast flag to signal the electronic device receiving the digital broadcast that content may not be redistributed in another form, such as over the Internet. Technology industry officials in a broadcast unit of the CPTWG group said that they were set to finalize the technical standards for such a flag by the end of March 2002. Officials at Intel, which has taken the lead in opposing the Hollings legislation because of it interjection of the government in its engineering processes, recently agreed with AOL Time Warner that some narrowly focused government regulation will be necessary; presumably from the FCC.

But solving this broadcast flag program was only the first of three demands that Motion Picture Association of America President Jack Valenti set in his February testimony before the Senate Commerce Committee. The second calls for plugging what he called the analog hole, or the analog output device on the back of television equipment. Even when video content is delivered in an encrypted digital format, it must be converted into an unprotected analog format to be viewed on existing analog televisions, and viewers may then convert it back to a digital form through which it could be sent transmitted to a Napster-like file-sharing service-so that it will be garbled whenever copied to another device–and would not be as straightforward as the motion picture industry believes.

The industry is nearly apoplectic over the third demand, which appears to drive the sweeping nature of Hollings' 2038: (that the technology industry do something to develop unspecified technical solutions that would counter the ability of someone to use computers, software, or electronic equipment to make an authorized copy available through a file-sharing service). Many share the view that Princeton professor Edward Felten expressed in written testimony to the Commerce Committee: "A standard for copy protection is as premature as a standard for teleportation". Intel CEO Craig Barrett said that he is aware of no technology that could do what MPAA wants done, short of monitoring every electronic communication and comparing bit streams to those of all known or registered copyrighted content.

2. DMCA

The debate over the Hollings bill has united the technology, consumer electronics and Internet rights communities against Hollywood. Among those leading the charge against the bill are the Business Software alliance, Computer Systems Policy Project, the Information Technology Industry Council, all of who represent the largest players in the software and hardware industries. Many of the same companies, particularly leading lights in the Business Software Alliance such as Microsoft and Adobe, played a key role in lending support to the DMCA. They now argue against Hollings' bill on a number of grounds: that it presumes bad faith on the part of the technology industry, that it gets government involved in the technology standards-setting process, that it would mandate a single digital rights management technology instead of permitting competing ones to flourish, and that by doing so it would inevitably freeze technological development (Clark, 2002).

But they also argue that privately created standards must be enforced with bars on circumvention, or "locks for digital doors". Without legal infrastructure, they countered; their efforts to secure content via encryption would come to naught as soon as the first crack is made available on the Internet. Not having the DMCA would grant too much flexibility to software pirates in a world where a single digital copy obtained via circumvention could be reproduced countless times.

Sophisticated defenders of the DMCA position also make another point as well. In addition to greatly facilitating unauthorized copying, the emergence of an Internet that is always on enables new sorts of access to copyrighted content. Instead of a world in which optical disk factories print CD-ROMs, we are moving to a world where software services that are consumed on high-speed Internet connections not by means of reproduction, but by having the proper access control to the service. In this view of world, a thief is not a pirate who has copied software but a hacker who publicizes the password to the service.

Without the anti-circumvention provisions, the business models of the future would not happen. Among these services are DVD's pay-per-view movies on subscription-based cable and satellite services, digital music web casting, and libraries of digital music pre-installed on the hard disks of computers sold through retailers.

But DMCA critics counter that copyright holders made the argument that there would be greater content if there were more protection–which is also being pressed by proponents of the Hollings' bill–before the DMCA's passage, and yet digital music and digital video services remain stalled.

3. Fair Use

However, advocates of the fair use doctrine emphasize how much the DMCA upsets traditional habits and patterns of copyright use from the perspective of the user. Among those who hold this view are manufacturers who benefit from the sale of consumer electronics products, internet Service Providers who saw demand for bandwidth skyrocket during the rise of Napster from July 2000 until the 9th Circuit Court of Appeals ruled that it was engaging in contributory and vicarious copyright infringement in February 2001, librarians who want greater access to copyrighted material, and consumers who believe that the balance in copyright law has swung away too far from consumers. One strong new representation of this view is a group dubbed Digital Consumer.org, founded by Joe Kraus, a former co-founder of Excite At Home, the Internet portal and broadband company that filed for bankruptcy September 2001 (Clark, 2002). The group, which includes many technology industry and venture capital luminaries, is attempting to put content owners on the defensive by asserting a six-point Bill of Rights with regard to consumers' use of digital materials:

- Users have the right to time-shift content that they have legally acquired. This gives consumers the right to record video or audio for later viewing or listening. For example, consumers may use a VCR to record a TV show and play it back later.

- Users have the right to space-shift content that they have legally acquired. This gives consumers the right to use your content in different places (as long as each use is personal and non-commercial). For example, consumers can coy a CD to a portable music player so that one can listen to the songs while jogging.

- Users have the right to make back-up copies for their content. This gives consumers the right to make archival copies to be used in the event that one's copies are destroyed.

- Users have the right to use legally acquired content on the platform of their choice. This gives consumer the right to listen to music on a Rio, to watch TV on an iMac, and to view DVDs on a Linux computer.

- Users have the right to translate legally acquired content into comparable formats. This gives consumer the right to modify content in order to make it more usable. For example, a blind person may modify an electronic book so that the content can be read out loud.

- Users have the right to use technology in order to achieve the rights previously mentioned. This last right guarantees consumers ability to exercise their other rights. Certain recent copyright laws have paradoxical loopholes that claim to grant certain rights but then criminalize all technologies that could allow consumers to exercise those rights. In contrast, this Bill of Rights states that no technological barriers can deprive consumers of their other fair use rights.

Principle one, regarding time-shifting, is controversial and flows directly from 1984 supreme court decision in Universal v. Sony Betamzx, which upheld the sale of videocassette recorders, including its use by consumers to make copies of copyrighted television and move programs. Regarding principle three, provisions of copyright law already permit backup copies of software but not digital music files. (Music file-backup would be included under one of the changes contemplated by H.R.2724, the Music Online Competition Act introduced by Rep. Chris Cannon, R-Utah, and Rep. Boucher.) But principles two, four, and five – each dealing with some form of altering copyrighted material to suit other formats or devices are opposed by many copyright interests. And are particularly critical of principle six, which essentially calls for a 'fair use' exception to the DMCA along the lines proposed by Boucher.

Content holders argue that these positions are based on an excessively broad rating of fair use–as understood by some consumers, perhaps, but not by copyright law. They also point to two studies conducted by the Library of Congress's Copyright Office, which rebutted the notion that the DMCA was responsible for limiting consumers' fair use access to material and rejecting almost all calls for exceptions to the anti-circumvention language.

Noting that fair use is a defense against infringement and not an affirmative right to copy, the more extreme among the copyright maximalists actually argue that fair use extends to quotation and parody, not to home and personal copies. They also argue that these broad definitions of fair use sanction those who would justify the use of Napster-like services on such grounds.

4. Free Speech

Most fair use defenders including Boucher, DigitalConsumer.com, and many consumer electronics companies, blanch at defending the old Napster. But free speech advocates – as exemplified by the EFF, many copyright law professors, and computer scientists-will rise to the occasion and argue that P2P services should not be shut down whether or not the infringing activity is conducted by individual users of such services (Clark, 2002).

Perhaps of even greater concern for this group, including librarians, are the DMCA's restrictions on what they see as legitimate scientific research and other activities chilled by the DMCA. Just as cryptographers sought to publish research about and deploy strong encryption free from government export restriction, they oppose private efforts to use the DMCA to quash investigations that could lead to breaking the encryption algorithms used by copyright holders. And they can point to a precedent in the 1999 9th Circuit Court of Appeals decision in Bernstein v. U.S. Department of State, upholding a mathematician's view that source code was protected as speech under the First Amendment.

Georgetown University Law Professor Julie Cohen, for example, has argued that fair use is an intrinsic part of copyright law and that private digital rights management technologies must not override it. Chapman University Law Professor Tom Bell takes the opposite track, suggesting that absent the DMCA- nothing should preclude content companies from restricting the copying of their intangible creations. Instead, the focus should be on 'escaping copyright law' and relying exclusively on private contractual remedies against copying. And Stanford University Law Professor Lawrence Lessig directs much of his criticism about copyright law to the length of its terms. (Lessing is attorney for Eric Edlred, the electronic book publisher challenging the Copyright Term Extension Act's 20-year bequest to current and future copyright holders, and argued the case before Supreme Court in October 2002). He states that if the law limited copyright holders for five years upto registration- renewable for up to 95 years – then the public domain would benefit from a huge influx of materials that are currently being locked out of it for no apparent benefit.

IV. Surveys

1. Survey.Net

Survey-Net is *the* source for user demographics on the Internet. It invites anyone to participate in online surveys. The information accumulated online is available to everyone on the net. It is free to republish/use any portion of the survey results as long as it is acknowledged (Source: http://www.survey.net/ip0r.html).

1. Online Intellectual Property Survey. Survey started: May 23, 2000 (in-progress).

Total Respondents: 1462 as of July 9, 2002 (Survey Consent Form-Appendix B).

<u>**Questionnaire:**</u>

What is your age?

	%	Count	Age
	19.4%	284	**22-25**
	14.1%	206	**26-30**
	9.4%	137	**16-17**
	9.0%	131	**31-35**
	6.6%	96	**36-40**
	5.7%	84	**Under 15**
	5.7%	83	**20**
	5.7%	83	**21**
	5.3%	77	**41-45**
	4.9%	71	**18**
	4.8%	70	**19**
	3.6%	52	**46-50**
	2.5%	37	**51-55**
	1.3%	19	**No Answer**
	0.9%	13	**56-60**
	0.3%	5	**61-65**
	0.3%	5	**66-70**
	0.3%	5	**81+**
	0.1%	2	**71-80**

What is your sex?

	%	Count	Sex
	53.7%	785	**Male**
	42.2%	617	**Female**
	4.0%	58	**No Answer**

Your highest level of education completed:

	%	Count	Education
	22.2%	324	**Some college**
	20.1%	294	**College - currently enrolled**
	18.9%	276	**College - Bachelors degree**

14.4% 210 **Some high school**

10.1% 148 **High school graduate**

8.4% 123 **College - Masters degree**

3.1% 46 **College – PhD**

2.7% 39 **No Answer**

Have you ever done any of the following:

78.2% 1143 **downloaded an image off the internet-not knowing if it was copyrighted**

70.1% 1025 **let a friend borrow an audio cd/tape to make a copy**

59.8% 874 **let a friend borrow your program disks to install software**

54.4% 796 **downloaded a MP3 file of a popular song without paying a fee**

49.5% 723 **downloaded an image off the internet that was copyrighted**

37.8% 552 **burned an unauthorized cd containing copyrighted material**

36.3% 531 **downloaded a MIDI file of a popular song without paying a fee**

26.8% 392 **built a web page using images or content from another web site without permission**

17.1% 250 **transferred a copyrighted file via ICQ**

Have you ever bought an album/cd that you first heard about after obtaining an illegal digital copy?

59.4% 869 **No**

38.0% 555 **Yes**

2.5% 36 **No Answer**

Have you ever purchased a software title after originally obtaining an unauthorized/pirated copy?

64.4% 942 **No**

32.0% 468 **Yes**

3.4% 50 **No Answer**

Have you ever obtained a commercial software program from the net without paying for it?

61.3% 896 **No**

35.8% 524 **Yes**

2.7% 40 **No Answer**

Have you ever registered or "cracked" a program with an unauthorized key or serial number?

68.0% 994 **No**
29.1% 426 **Yes**
2.7% 40 **No Answer**

Do you use any of the following software?

64.6% 944 **Microsoft Media Player**
53.7% 785 **Quicktime**
41.1% 601 **Napster**
39.9% 583 **Winamp**
32.4% 473 **ICQ**
23.9% 350 **Onlinemp3**
18.6% 272 **MusicMatch Jukebox**
10.7% 156 **IRC**

Do you think web pages should be copyrighted and protected as intellectual property?

49.5% 723 **Yes**
44.7% 653 **No**
5.7% 84 **No Answer**

Do you believe digital IMAGE files should be afforded the same protections in cyberspace as their offline counterparts?

48.3% 706 **Yes**
44.0% 644 **No**
7.5% 110 **No Answer**

Do you believe digital AUDIO files should be afforded the same protections in cyberspace as their offline counterparts?

47.9% 700 **Yes**
46.0% 672 **No**
6.0% 88 **No Answer**

Do you have any copyrighted material (images, audio files, software, or other data) that you downloaded from the net to your hard drive without specific permission?

49.2%　720　**Yes**

44.5%　651　**No**

6.1%　89　**No Answer**

Do you have any copyrighted material (images, audio files, software, or other data) installed on your machine without a legitimate license?

50.2%　734　**No**

43.0%　629　**Yes**

6.6%　96　**No Answer**

Do you think companies that produce software such as Napster should be held responsible in one form or another for the illegal activities (piracy of copyrighted material) their software may facilitate?

63.5%　928　**No**

29.5%　432　**Yes**

6.5%　95　**No Answer**

Do you think there is a difference between software such as Napster, which helps people download MP3s regardless of whether they're copyrighted, and e-mail, usenet or other programs which afford similar abilities to acquire copyrighted material?

61.9%　905　**No**

28.0%　410　**Yes**

9.9%　145　**No Answer**

How would you rule in a case where an artist is suing a company that makes a program that facilitates easy copying of their material without remuneration?

46.6%　682　**I would dismiss the case because the company is simply creating a tool and is not responsible for its misuse**

14.6%　213　**I would force the company to work with the artist to identify and take action against copyright violators**

13.8%　202　**I would force the company to restrict illegal use of its product**

10.7%　157　**I would force the company to filter out artist's material from its system**

8.5%　125　**No Answer**

5.5%　81　**I would shut the software/company down**

The Survey.net survey, given below, included 53.8 percent of male and 42.0 percent female respondents between the ages of 22-30. 22.2 percent of the respondents had some college degree. The results of the survey indicate support for the hypothesis and theory of the study:

70.1% - let friend borrow an audio cd/tape to make a copy.

38.0% - bought an album/cd that they first heard about after obtaining an illegal digital copy.

31.9% - purchased a software title after originally obtaining a unauthorized/pirated copy.

35.9% - obtained a commercial software program from the net without paying for it.

29.2% - registered or 'cracked' a program with an unauthorized key or serial number.

44.5% - do not think web pages should be copyrighted and protected as intellectual property.

43.9% - believe digital IMAGE files should not be afforded the same protections in cyberspace as their offline counterparts.

45.9% - do not believe that digital AUDIO files should be afforded the same protections in cyberspace as their offline counterparts.

49.4% - have a copyrighted material (images, audio files, software, or other data) that they downloaded from the net to their hard drive without specific permission.

43.1% - do have copyrighted material (images, audio files, software, or other data) installed on a machine without a legitimate license.

63.5% - think companies that produce software such as Napster should be held responsible in one form or another for the illegal activities (piracy of copyrighted material their software may facilitate.

28.1% - think there is a difference between software such as Napster, which helps people download MP3s regardless of whether they are copyrighted, and email, usenet or other programs, which afford similar abilities to acquire copyrighted material.

46.7% - would rule in a case where an artist is suing a company that makes a program that facilitates easy copying of their material without remuneration.

2. Intellectual Property Law Survey

Intellectual Property Law Server. The intellectual property law server provides information about intellectual property law including patent, trademark, and copyright. Survey started: August 2000 (in-progress). Total Respondents: 2248 as of July 9, 2002 (Survey Consent Form-Appendix B). (Source: http://www.intelproplaw.com/?survey).

Questionnaire:

Should tools that make it very easy to breach copyright be illegal even though there may be some other legitimate use for those tools?

No: 73.93%
■
Yes: 20.24%
∎
Don't Know: 5.83%

Total Votes: 2248.

The IP Law Server Survey results revealed that 73.93 percent of the respondents indicated that the tools that make it very easy to breach copyright should not be illegal, even though there may be some other legitimate use for those tools that supports this study's hypothesis of having a balance between technology and legal framework for digital transactions.

The two research surveys consisted of a four-page document containing 18 questions. 16.66 percent of the questions are demographic. 33.33 percent of the questions are general questions relevant to the use of software and this study's theory. 50.00 percent of the questions are relevant to the hypothesis. The surveys consist of 12 yes/no questions. The results from two surveys support the hypothesis, theory, and analysis of the study.

V. Chapter Summary

The task of intellectual property protection has always been difficult, attempting as it does to achieve a finely tuned balance by: providing authors and publishers sufficient control over their work so that they are motivated to create and disseminate, while seeking to limit that control so that society as a whole benefits from access to the work. The emergence in the past 10 years of a new information infrastructure marked by the proliferation of personal computers, networks that connect them, and the World Wide Web have led to radical changes in how informational works are created and distributed, offering both enormous new opportunities and substantial challenges to the current model of intellectual property.

The information infrastructure creates both opportunities for and concerns about public access to information and archiving. Continuing the inquiry into the consequences of the information infrastructure for intellectual property, this chapter raised the question of whether the current regime of copyright will continue to be workable in the digital age or whether some of the basic legal models for intellectual property need to be re-conceptualized.

The chapter noted how the technology of digital information has vastly increased the ability of individuals to copy, produce, and distribute information, making the behavior of individuals and society a far more significant factor in the enforcement of IP rights than in the past. Yet apparently relatively little is known about the public's knowledge of or attitude to intellectual property.

The DMCA's anti-circumvention provision demonstrates the technology-specific nature of copyright law and suggests that it is challenging and perhaps difficult to draw the technological boundaries needed to sustain a coherent defense of copyright law, once one has accepted the premise of copyright law. It may well be that the weaknesses of the concept of copyright in a digital world make it hard to sustain a principled defense for the enshrinement of state power represented by IP copyright law.

The results of the content analysis and surveys also suggest that the four major positions about the proper scope for copyright in a digital world command some significant portion of the public debate, although none currently represents a consensus. This very fact of fluidity–with divergent views driven by the interests of the industries and professions that they represent-underscores the controversial nature of copyright law and suggests an opportune moment for rethinking exactly what it is that IP copyright is designed to protect and why and will be discussed in the next chapter, Interpretation, Conclusions and Recommendations.

Chapter 5: Interpretation, Conclusions, and Recommendations

I. Introduction

Intellectual property protection has always been a contentious field of study, but one largely left to lawyers and industry insiders. With the rise of the Internet commerce, however, IP disputes have become widespread, creating public interest and concern. Controversial issues and questions focus on the rights of authors, artists, and inventors over their intellectual creations.

Because of the controversy of copyrighted works, the questions addressed include the following queries: Is there a need to rework copyright incentives for promoting the useful arts? Should newer works receive the same copyright protection as the existing body of copyrighted material? Or can existing laws along with market solutions, such as digital rights management, protect copyrights? Is there still a role for compulsory licensing or has digitization taken away the market failure arguments that supported it in the past? Is the anti-circumvention provision of the Digital Millennium Copyright Act unconstitutional? And when does fair use become an illegal circumvention?

II. Review of the Problem

The purpose of this study is to examine how copyright issues and concerns were impacted by the arrival of eCommerce as outlined in the statement of the problem and the hypothesis developed in Chapter 1. The central research question concerned: why did the copyright become controversial with the introduction of commercial digital transactions? The analysis is accomplished through a review of the literature; Internet industry reports and IP related court cases. When tested with specific data, the study confirmed an association between the literature review and the researched data.

This study analyzes the need for generally agreed upon principles applicable to the technological measures used to identify, protect, and manage copyright works in the digital environment. An increased ability to protect intellectual property rights and to manage the distribution of copyright works over the Internet and other global methods of distribution will spur copyright-holders to produce more and copyright works available in digital environments.

Technology alone is not sufficient to protect copyrighted works from unauthorized reproduction and distribution. Legal safeguards and their enhancements, such as those required by the WIPO treaties and DMCA, must also be in place. This study strongly urges U.S. government officials to facilitate the establishment of open and globally harmonized common standards for technological protection of copyrighted works in the digital world.

This study finds that technological measures can be designed and used to accommodate certain exceptions in a rational and balanced way through the creation of special consumption rules for particular consumers or groups of beneficiaries. In addition, one benefit of technological protection measures is that, when effectively implemented they eliminate the need for and the legitimacy of copyright levies in those countries where such levies are imposed. Service providers should accommodate technological measures developed to monitor activities or identify infringing works provided these do not impose substantial costs on service providers or their systems and networks. Furthermore, the need for additional research on commerce laws, most specifically those related to DMCA, was identified. Seven propositions for the establishment and verification of the theory were developed.

III. Interpretation

a. Technological Protection Measures, Business Models, and DMCA

By linking the concept of anti-circumvention to copyright infringement, the DMCA raises new questions about the nature of copyright law. Originally designed to prevent copying, it now also constraints access, including access to materials that one has purchased such as a DVD or a computer. A fundamental change in copyright law is needed in order for successful eCommerce transactions.

In the previous chapter, many of the arguments of technology industry officials, and strong advocates of the DMCA, that were used to argue against Hollings S.2038, including the presumption of bad faith, putting government in the standards-setting business, mandating a single DRM technology, and freezing technological development were addressed. Additional concerns were that the fair use and free speech would oppose government imposition, even if a technological standard or standards were agreed upon by Hollywood and the technology industry. Unfettered copying–whether for fair use purposes or reproducing un-copyrighted materials, or for infringing purposes is not sanctioned by the manufacturers.

Many of the same objections against Holling's bill apply to DMCA. Many of the same arguments concerning S. 2048 seeking to write business models into the law apply equally to the DMCA. The benefits that flow from stronger copyright laws are obvious to copyright holders but do not count the costs to users, to economic welfare, and to free speech.

By criminalizing technologies used to circumvent copy-protection devices, the DMCA's Anti-circumvention provision adds significant new burdens to the already bloated corpus of copyright law. What were once minor constraints on the capabilities of content users to reproduce copyrighted material are increasingly more like an intolerable straightjacket that affect the way in which individuals enjoy and experience intangible creations.

Content copyright owners are loath to return to the pre-DMCA world. Increasingly copyright policy makers will be forced to choose which vision of the future they prefer: restrictions on digital devices in exchange for securing copyrights or technological freedom at the price of greater piracy. In either case, copyright law has lost its familiar grounding. In its short period of operation, the DMCA has already changed many fundamental perceptions about copyright law and turned many users of technology against copyright law. The DMCA and proposed new laws like the Consumer Broadband and Digital Television Promotion Act are the leading edge of these new digital restrictions. If copyright is to have a future in the digital world and for eCommerce to flourish, a better rationale is needed upon which to build future copyright policy.

New business models and technological innovations are rapidly transforming the way in which content providers create and distribute their works and offer consumers new and exciting means of receiving and enjoying these works. In addition, legal, business and technical challenges are also presented by the increasing use of peer-to-peer technologies.

The knowledge of the value of lawful use of protected works in stimulating the creative process supports a balanced approach that protects both the rights of content providers and the interests of various other parties. This approach reflects the fact that technological advances pose a challenge to those who create and /or distribute their works digitally and who are seeking to protect their works from unlawful reproduction and distribution. Widespread digital piracy of copyright works threatens to undermine online content distribution.

There is a need to embrace the technological innovations and commercial applications increasingly being made available in the marketplace. Industry is actively engaged in research and development that will continue to transform the business and technological landscape of the future. These new models and technologies give both consumers and content producers new tools to make informed choices about the content they consume and produce, as well as where, how, and on what devices they consume and distribute that content.

This study supports the development of technological measures that enable creators and rights-holders to employ new business models and that empower consumers to legally access and use the full range of diverse content available in the digital environment. Technological measures are designed to respond to content protection. Some may help rights-holders identify their works in digital environments, others may help them to protect their works and more easily distribute their works to authorized users.

Proprietary systems or architectures, or systems that reflect an approach pursued by a limited number of parties in voluntary private organizations, typically are subject to commercial agreements between private parties. Other technological measures may involve "open" systems and may be subject to broad industry agreement or standardization. All of these types of measures will potentially prove useful in facilitating the legal access and use of copyrighted content.

Internet commerce supports a secure environment in which legitimate copyright content distribution can flourish. Software developers, artists, musicians, writers, filmmakers, animators, game developers, and copyrights-holders invest substantial time and resources in the creation of their art and products and in mastering their craft. The creation and production of copyright works require substantial financial investments, which are typically recouped through licensing of uses of the work or the sale of copies.

Network operators have substantial investments in the infrastructure and services that support the Internet. They are also interested in ensuring that the integrity of the networks is not compromised. A stable and secure environment supports online content distribution by reaching an industry wide consensus on open and globally harmonized technological content protection standards. All relevant stakeholders needs are addressed.

To ensure that access to and use of copyright works is legitimate and that the rights of content providers are fully respected, it is necessary to manage the usage and exploitation of copyrighted works. A widely agreed upon industry-developed standard for technological measures coupled with an appropriate legal framework that achieves full implementation of the WIPO Copyright and Performances and Phonograms Treaties of 1996 (WIPO Treaties) are essential elements for the effective protection of intellectual property rights in the digital environment.

The various types of technological measures permit content copyright owners to offer consumers works in higher quality formats (such as DVD and enhanced definition TV) and to receive the works over a wider array of distribution channels and at various price points. Cross-sectoral multi-industry efforts to develop and deploy standard technological measures will ensure that they fulfill their purposes without imposing unreasonable financial or operational burdens on equipment manufacturers, service providers or the efficient operation of communication networks.

Technology, even when robust or reliable, is subject to attack from hackers and pirates. For this reason, technology alone is not sufficient to protect copyright works from unauthorized reproduction and distribution. Legal safeguards and their enhancements, such as those required by the WIPO Treaties and improved version of DMCA, must be in place to support technological measures and prohibit unlawful duplication. Requirements to prohibit the circumvention of these technologies are a central feature of the WIPO Treaties.

The U.S. Government should promptly ratify the WIPO Treaties and implement appropriate legal frameworks for effective technological protection measures. Such legislation should also prohibit circumvention-related activities by regulating both copyrighted conduct and devices, while providing appropriate exceptions, such as those set forth in the U.S. DMCA of 1998, that maintain the overall balance between copyright-holders, service providers, and users.

There are multiple business models being pursued to offer digital content, and several private cross-sectional industry-wide negotiations regarding open standard setting processes are underway that relate to technological measures. These include TV-Anytime, MPEG, and CSS, to name a few. Because technological measures often require a degree of implementation by content copyright owners, service providers, and equipment manufacturers to function effectively, cross-sectoral multi-industry recognition and licensing arrangements are essential to facilitate enforcement.

The tradition of providing for a limited degree of access to published materials that was established in the world of physical artifacts must be continued in the digital context. But the mechanisms for achieving this access and the definition of limited degree will need to evolve in response to the attributes of digital intellectual property and the information infrastructure. The confluence of three developments-the changing nature of publication in the digital world, the increasing use of licensing rather than sale, and the use of technical protection services-creates unprecedented opportunities for individuals to access information in improved and novel ways, but also could have a negative impact on public access to information. Developments over time should be monitored closely.

The information infrastructure has blurred the distinction between publication and private distribution. An important underlying legal and philosophical issue with respect to the question of whether fair use is an affirmative right or a defense-and emphasizes the consequences for access that follow from taking one position or the other on this issue. Significant economic, technical, and legal issues need to be resolved if libraries and archiving institutions are to be as successful with digital information as they have been with hard-copy information. When commercial enterprises add value to basic data, the resulting products deserve copyright protection insofar as these products otherwise satisfy the legal requirements for copyright. A better understanding is needed of the public's perception and behavior concerning digital intellectual property. When popular attitudes and practices are out of synch with laws, the enforcement of laws becomes more difficult, which may instill in people a lack of confidence in and respect for the legal system. There are also political dangers associated with criminalizing generally accepted behavior, given the possibilities for discriminatory and selective enforcement.

It is important to find ways to convince the public to consider thoughtfully the legality, ethics, and economic implications of their acts of private copying. Fair use and other exceptions to copyright law derive from the fundamental purpose of copyright law and the concomitant balancing of competing interests among stakeholder groups. Although the evolving information infrastructure changes the processes by which fair use and other exceptions to copyright are achieved, it does not challenge the underlying public policy motivations. Thus, fair use and other exceptions to copyright law should continue to play a role in the digital environment. Providing additional statutory limitations on copyright and/or additional statutory protections may be necessary over time to adapt copyright appropriately to the digital environment. The fair use doctrine may also prove useful as a flexible mechanism for adapting copyright to the digital environment.

A better understanding of the basic principles of copyright law would lead to greater respect for this law and greater willingness to abide by it, as well as produce a more informed public better able to engage in discussions about intellectual property and public policy. Technical protection services need not be perfect to be useful. Most people are not technically knowledgeable enough to defeat even moderately sophisticated systems and, in any case, are law-abiding citizens rather than determined adversaries. Technical protection technologies are currently deployed to varying degrees. Some, such as encryption and password protection, are widely deployed. Others, such as Web monitoring, watermarking, time stamping, and rights-management, are well developed but not yet widely deployed. Copy prevention techniques are deployed to a limited degree. The copy prevention mechanism used in digital video disks provides a notable example of mature development and consumer market penetration.

Systems that have been commercialized to date require a substantial infrastructure to manage secure identification of users or authorization of actions. As cryptography is frequently a crucial enabling technology for technical protection services, continued advances in technical protection services require a productive and leading-edge community of cryptography and security researchers and developers. Some digital information may be distributed more securely using physical substrates rather than by computer networks.

More legitimate reasons to circumvent access control systems exist than are currently recognized in the Digital Millennium Copyright Act. For example, a copyright owner might need to circumvent an access control system to investigate whether someone else is hiding infringement by encrypting a copy of that owner's works, or a firm might need to circumvent an access control system to determine whether a computer virus was about to infect its computer system. Both technology and business models can serve as effective means for deriving value from digital intellectual property. Technical protection mechanisms can reduce the rate of unauthorized use of IP, but impose their own costs (in production, service, and sometimes customer effort). An appropriate business model can sometimes sharply reduce the need for technical protection; yet provide a way to derive substantial value from IP. Models that can accomplish this objective range from a traditional sales model (low-priced, mass market distribution with convenient purchasing, where the low price and ease of purchase make buying more attractive than copying), to the more radical step of giving away IP and selling a complementary product or service.

While recognizing that no one technological measure, business model and legal framework can respond to the requirements of all stakeholders, the outlined general conclusions listed below are intended to promote the development of standard technological measures to identify, protect and manage various forms of content in various environments and physical locations irrespective of the media on which it is stored. The delivery systems by which it is transmitted, accessed or made available (e.g., TV, Internet, etc.) and the equipment or device by which it is received, displayed, recorded or transferred (e.g., TV sets, PCs, handheld devices, etc.) are outlined in the conclusions.

IV. Conclusions and Research Contributions

The results of the study indicate that both the primary and secondary data supported the research hypothesis that if legal rules are not set and applied appropriately, information technology has the potential to undermine the basic tenets of copyright. Furthermore, a reasoned and fact-based dialogue drives policy-making on questions about the sale of copies of programs, software, music, art, books, and movies.

In addition, the entertainment industry will eventually use the Internet as a means of reaching out to millions of consumers they otherwise would not have for future economic benefits and public good. The analysis and interpretation of the results led to the following seven *conclusions*:

1. Anti-Circumvention and Copyright Management Information – The addition of new sections to the Copyright Act are required to implement the World Intellectual Property Organization Copyright Treaty and the WIPO Performances and Phonograms Treaty. A person who circumvents technological copy protections commits copyright infringements. Additionally, individuals who knowingly provide false copyright management information or who remove copyright management information without the authority of the copyright owner should be held liable and accountable for such acts.

2. Fair Use -- Current copyright law permits copyrighted material to be copied or shared without compensation under certain circumstances, such as copying for personal use, or copying to promote the creation and distribution of new, non-infringing works. Amendments in the copyright law are required to make clear that the fair use doctrine continues to apply with full force in the digital network environment.

3. Temporary Copies -- Several proposals offered by copyright owners make temporary, or ephemeral, reproductions created in computers or other devices in the operation of digital information networks, violations of copyright law. One result of such violations could mean that "browsing" the Internet would be illegal since it has become a common practice by all computer literates. Amendments in the copyright law are required to make explicit that no infringement has taken place when a person makes a digital copy of a copyright protected work provided such copying is incidental to the operation of a computer, or other device, as part of a digital information network.

4. First Sale -- Under current law, an individual who has legally obtained a book or videocassette may transfer it to another person without permission of the copyright owner. A "digital equivalent" of the first sale doctrine is required to permit electronic transmission of a work in certain circumstances.

5. Pre-emption – Amendments in the federal law are required that preclude copyright owners from using non-negotiable "shrink-wrap," the listed license terms are agreed to when the multimedia or software product is opened, licenses to take away rights consumers otherwise would enjoy under the current copyright law.

6. Distance Learning – Amendments in the copyright law are required to ensure that educators are able to use personal computers and new technology legally to educate individuals without violating copyright laws.

7. Library Exemptions – Amendments are required to facilitate the use of digital and new technology for archiving purposes.

Study's Contribution:

The development and implementation of effective standard technological measures are an ongoing process that will require the cooperation of all relevant stakeholders. New online business models and effective technological measures are useful tools to continue the expansion of eCommerce over the Internet. Effective technological measures and legal safeguards can solve the sub-problems as stated in Chapter 1. They will also protect unlawful circumvention and are an important means by which intellectual property can be identified, protected, and delivered securely.

Confluence of Computers, Internet (eCommerce), and IP (Copyright)

Based on the scope and limitations of the study to date outlined in Chapter 1, this study attempted to make its valuable contribution to human knowledge by the following:

1. extending and synthesizing the works of WIPO on *copyright* and currently available related eCommerce and intellectual property literature;

2. extending and synthesizing the works of the Information Infrastructure Task Force report *Intellectual Property and the National Information Infrastructure* (IITF Paper, 1995) in addressing protection technologies and technological measures;

3. extending and synthesizing the works of Hardy's (1998) report, *Future of Copyright in the Networked World in* addressing online business models;

4. extending and synthesizing the works of the NAP (2000) report on the *'Digital Dilemma'* solely from copyright perspective in providing conclusions;

5. extending and synthesizing the works of Clark's (2002) argument *"How Copyright Became Controversial" in* providing recommendations;

6. suggesting guidelines for further research; and

7. suggesting directions to policy makers on how successful commercial digital transactions over the Internet are to be carried out in the coming years.

It is widely known that producing photocopies of a textbook and distributing them to others are not lawful. This is because the WIPO Copyright Treaty, states that authors of such literary works enjoy the exclusive right of authorizing the making available to the public copies of their works. In other words, no one but the author (or the owner of the copyright, as the case may be) has the right to make such copies of the work.

Computer programs in the form of software, according to the WIPO Copyright Treaty, are protected exactly as literary works are protected under Article 2 of the Berne Convention for Protection of Artistic and Literary Works. This means that the copyright privileges that literary and artistic works enjoy extend to computer programs as well. Therefore, only the owner of the copyright itself enjoys the exclusive right of making copies of the computer program available to the public.

The same principle applies to computer games, a more specific type of computer software. The US copyright law states that although the idea for a game is not protected by copyright, the manner of expression of the author (in artistic, literary, or musical form) is protected. Therefore, it is unlawful to distribute copies of computer games without the copyright owner's explicit permission.

Works made available to the public on the Internet are also protected by copyright. For works made available over a communications network (such as the Internet), the copyright protects original authorship. This, of course, applies only to those who wish to obtain the copyright. But just as limitations exist with games, the copyrighting of online works, according to the U.S. Copyright Law, does not protect *ideas, procedures, systems,* or *methods of operation*. This means that once an online work has been made public, nothing in the copyright laws prevents others from developing another work based on similar principles or ideas.

Although these exceptions to the rules make interpretations and applications more difficult, with the increasing popularity of computers, the growth of the Internet and eCommerce, matters have become more complex. New situations arise daily and copyright laws currently available are not adequate to deal with them. Traditional copyright laws often seem outdated in the ever-changing technological world. Because the present copyright laws do not clearly define what should be done in such cases, controversy is often the result.

Furthermore, issues involving copyright laws and computers tend to become rather complex, so it is not at all surprising that controversy often arises in this novel area of computer ethics. The most controversial areas in Internet cases seem to be those involving copyright laws. An issue that has become fundamental to computer usage and computer ethics, therefore, is copyright protection.

In general, the following general rules are likely to resolve the copy ownership problem:

1. If one produced the work oneself, then one is the natural author and owner of the copyright.

2. If one is an employee who has created the work in the scope of employment, one's employer owns the copyright and is in fact considered the author.

The U.S. copyright law provides a more elaborate list of rules governing the ownership of copyright. Therefore, when examining copyright ownership, the following issues should always be considered:

1. Who is the natural author? Who produced the work?

2. Is the creation a work for his/her employee?

3. Is the creation a work for him/her as a specially commissioned work?

4. Is the person a joint author of the work?

5. Has the person obtained a valid license to use the copyrighted work?

6. Are the rights that the person has obtained recognizable and enforceable under the current law?

To sum up, it is not legal to use others' work without explicit permission from the owner of the work's copyright. Copyright infringement constitutes the reproduction of a work without such express permission. It is important to note, however, that the reproduced work need not be *identical* to the original work. If the copied work is substantially similar to the original, it is considered to have infringed upon the copyright of the original.

At the time of this study, rulings provided by the courts have not fully elucidated the relationship between copyright laws and Internet. That is, there exist no explicit guidelines to follow in cases involving these two areas. Internet users must wait for better decisions. But with the development of a new medium such as the World Wide Web, it is not surprising that a new definition for copyright must be developed. New questions regarding intellectual property have arisen, and a crucial balance between the positive and detrimental effects of this technology must be found.

The results of this study provide new insights on theoretical perspectives on intellectual property and the impact of eCommerce in a virtual environment. Most studies on intellectual property have studied primarily face-to-face interactions in various settings, whereas the virtual character of the Internet adds yet another point of interest to human interaction. As society shifts increasingly towards Internet-mediated communication, it will be crucial to investigate the impact of intellectual property in such settings.

There is great diversity in the kinds of digital intellectual property, business models, legal mechanisms, and technical protection services possible, making a one-size-fits-all solution too rigid. Currently a wide variety of new models and mechanisms are being created, tried out, and in some cases discarded, at a furious pace. This process should be supported and encouraged, to allow all parties to find models and mechanisms well suited to their needs. Law and public policy must be crafted to consider all the relevant forces in the digital environment. Initiatives that consider or rely on only one or a subset of the relevant forces are not likely to serve the nation well. Policy makers must conceive of and analyze issues in a manner that is as technology-independent as possible, drafting policies and legislation in a similar fashion. The question to focus on is not so much exactly what device is causing the problem today, as what the underlying issue is. Nor should policy makers base their decisions on the specifics of any particular business model.

Public compliance with intellectual property law requires a high degree of simplicity, clarity, straightforwardness, and comprehensibility for all aspects of copyright law that deal with individual behavior. New or revised intellectual property laws should be drafted accordingly. The movement toward clarity and specificity in the law must also preserve a sufficient flexibility and adaptability so that the law can accommodate technologies and behaviors that may evolve in the future as suggested in more detail in the next section, Recommendations for Further Research.

V. Recommendations for Future Research

Representatives from government, rights holders, publishers, libraries, and other cultural heritage institutions, the public, and technology providers should convene to begin a discussion of models for public access to information that are mutually workable in the context of the widespread use of licensing and technical protection services. The concept of publication should be reevaluated and clarified by the various stakeholder groups in response to the fundamental changes caused by the information infrastructure. The public policy implications of a new concept of publication should also be determined.

Congress should investigate enacting legislation to permit copying of digital information for archival purposes, whether the copy is in the same format or migrated to a new format. As a general principle, the basic data created or collected by the federal government should be available at a modest cost, usually not to exceed the direct costs associated with distribution of the data. When agencies contract with a commercial enterprise to make federally supported primary data available and provide no other mechanism for access to the data, such agreements should provide for public access at a cost that does not exceed the direct costs associated with distribution.

Research and data collection should be pursued to develop a better understanding of what types of digital copying people think are permissible, what they regard as infringements, and what falls into murky ill-defined areas. Such research should address how these views differ from one community to another, how they differ according to type of material (e.g., software, recorded music, online documents), how user behavior follows user beliefs, and to what extent further knowledge about copyright law is likely to change user behavior.

Legal, economic, and public policy research should be undertaken to help determine the extent to which fair use and other exceptions and limitations to copyright should apply in the digital environment. As public policy research, legal developments, and the marketplace shape the scope of fair use and other limitations on copyright, and/or demonstrate a need for additional protections, any additional actions that may be needed to adapt the law, educate the public about it, or enforce the law may become clearer. An educational program should be undertaken that emphasizes the benefits that copyright law provides to all parties. Such a copyright education program needs to be planned and executed with care.

Rights holders might consider using technical protection services to help manage digital intellectual property but should also bear in mind the potential for diminished public access and the costs involved, some of which are imposed on customers and society. In addition to the currently required Librarian of Congress study of some of the impacts of the Digital Millennium Copyright Act's anticircumvention provisions, broader assessments should be conducted of the impacts of the anticircumvention provisions of the DMCA as a whole. This broader review of the regulations is justified because of their unprecedented character; their breadth; and widespread concerns about their potential for negative impacts on public access to information, on the ability of legitimate users to make noninfringing uses of copyrighted works, on research and development in security technology, and on competition and innovation in the high-technology sector. This review should occur periodically and should include a study of impacts of the antidevice provisions of the DMCA.

Rights holders should give careful consideration to the power that business models offer for dealing with distribution of digital information. The judicious selection of a business model may significantly reduce the need for technical protection or legal protection, thereby lowering development and enforcement costs. But the model must be carefully matched to the product: While the appropriate business model can for some products obviate the need for technical protection, for others (e.g., first-run movies) substantial protection may be necessary (and even the strongest protection mechanisms likely to be available soon may be inadequate).

Legislators should not contemplate a major overhaul of intellectual property laws and public policy at this time to permit the evolutionary process the time to play out. Research should be initiated to better assess the social and economic impacts of illegal commercial copying and how they interact with private noncommercial copying for personal use. Research should be conducted to characterize the economic impacts of copyright. Such research might consider, among other things, the impact of network effects in information industries and how digital networks are changing transaction costs. Research should be conducted to ensure that expansion of patent protection for information inventions is aligned with the constitutional intent of promoting the progress of science and the useful arts. Legal research should be undertaken on the status of temporary reproductions and derivative work rights to inform the process of adapting copyright law to the digital environment, and to assist policy makers and judges in their deliberations.

Research should be undertaken in the areas that are most likely to intersect with intellectual property law, namely, contract law, communications policy, privacy policy, and First Amendment policy. The interaction of intellectual property law and contract law is likely to be of particular significance in the relatively near future, as licensing becomes a more common means of information distribution, leading to potential conflicts with the goals of IP law. An exploration of whether or not the notion of copy is an appropriate foundation for copyright law, and whether a new foundation can be constructed for copyright, based on the goal set forth in the Constitution ("promote the progress of science and the useful arts") and a tactic by which it is achieved, namely, providing incentive to authors and publishers. In this framework, the question would not be whether a copy had been made, but whether a use of a work was consistent with the goal and tactic (i.e., did it contribute to the desired progress and was it destructive, when taken alone or aggregated with other similar copies, of an author's incentive). This concept is similar to fair use but broader in scope, as it requires considering the range of factors by which to measure the impact of the activity on authors, publishers, and others.

Based on the interpretation and conclusions of the study, five recommendations for further research are offered that are designed to achieve the goal of maintaining the proper balance between ownership and access rights for eCommerce:

1. Standardization

Research efforts are needed to adopt technological measures voluntarily through the use of private commercial agreements, and also by industry-led and /or Government-facilitated standardization processes. Standardized technological measures developed and mutually agreed upon by a broad multi-industry group of stakeholders in an open, fair, and voluntary standards setting process are required. Government facilitation is needed for the development of open and globally harmonized technological content protection standards.

2. Rights Holders

National copyright laws often provide for certain exceptions to the rights of copyright-holders. According to the Berne Convention, the TRIPS Agreement, and the WIPO Treaties, these exceptions may only be provided for in certain special cases that do not conflict with the normal exploitation of the work and do not unreasonably prejudice the legitimate interests of the author or related rights-holder. Further researched is needed regarding some concerns about the decisions of rights holders. For example, whether or not and how to bring suit against technological measures that compromise the ability of consumers and other groups of beneficiaries to benefit from copyright exceptions. In addition, the use of technological measures to maximize choice, facilitate greater availability of content in new formats and distribution channels to benefit consumers.

Technological measures are evolving to accommodate certain exceptions in a rational and balanced way through the creation of special consumption rules for particular consumers or groups of beneficiaries. Content owners have interests in making their works available, using various business models to the widest audience possible. Content that remains locked away does not generate value for its creator or for others in the value chain. The technological measures to facilitate right-holders' abilities to identify and manage the dissemination of their works in existing and new distribution channels, and will help prevent unlawful reproduction, distribution, (re) publication, and (re) transmission. Such measures also lead to the growth of business models in which right-holders can seek different levels of compensation directly from consumers for different uses of their works and opportunities to legally access and use those works can be enhanced. Other stakeholders involved in the distribution of digital content, including service and infrastructure providers, can also benefit from such measures.

Technological measures to enhance the tools available to rights-holders to manage their rights in accordance with public interests will play a critical role in promoting more convenient and wider distribution and communication of works to consumers, while taking account of the concerns of network operators and other stakeholders. Exceptions or limitations to anti-circumvention obligations is focused narrowly to preserve the adequacy and effectiveness of the anti-circumvention prohibitions. Exceptions to anti-circumvention obligations are not to be so broad as to undermine the basic prohibition, or to permit the sale or distribution of circumventing devices to the public.

Also, those outright exceptions to anti-circumvention provisions are not the only way to maintain the policies behind copyright exceptions and limitations. Other techniques are needed including the establishment of a mechanism for ongoing government supervision to ensure that technological measures are not used in such a way that they adversely affect lawful uses of copyrighted works.

3 Copyright Levies

Copyright levies are imposed by some national governments in order to attempt to compensate rights-holders for legal private copies of their works made by consumers. The development and deployment of technological measures increasingly enable rights-holders to establish direct relationships with customers and directly track and manage the legal use and copying of their copyright works. One of the clear benefits of technological protection measures is that, elimination of the need for, and the legitimacy of, copyright levies in those countries where such levies are imposed. The rapid development and deployment of effective technological measures is needed to avoid the proliferation of new copyright levies that could have a potentially negative impact on economic growth, business investments, and global competitiveness and potentially undermine remunerative business models.

4. Copyright Management Technologies

Some types of copy control technologies, such as watermarks, embed within the content itself copy control and content management information that travels with the content from end-to-end (from initial distribution to end-user consumption). These technologies are designed to ensure that content is protected at all points along the distribution chain throughout its commercial lifecycle. Technologies can be effective in preventing unlawful access and copying if appropriately responded to by playback and recording devices, and if their integrity is not compromised and if they are not rendered ineffective before the content reaches the end-user. Watermark technologies, supplemented where necessary with other types of copy management encryption technology, help to ensure that content is protected. These can include, for example, digital rights management systems, designed to enable multiple usage models including secure peer-to-peer technology, to facilitate payments to rights-holders, and to provide protection against copyright infringements. Cross-sectoral industry-wide discussions, development, and negotiations are needed to reach agreements on standard consensus technologies.

5. Availability and Access

Standard technological measures adopted and established to identify, protect, and manage copyright works, wherever possible, allow for interoperability with other technological measures and function over a wide range of equipment and distribution channels. Where possible, standard technological measures are needed for interacting with each other to preserve the integrity of copy protection and management information that accompanies with the content, and the integrity and efficiency of network operations. Further research is needed for standard technological measures established to identify, protect, and manage copyright works for sufficiently extensible (meaning not static and incapable of extensions) and flexible to ensure that new technological developments can be accommodated and that business models can evolve.

With standard technological measures and specifications to be agreed upon, solutions are to be implemented and made commercially available. Standard technological measures, offered by the developers or copyright owners, are to be widely available on fair, reasonable, and non-discriminatory terms for implementation by all relevant stakeholders. Technological measure and distribution methods are needed to evolve in order to provide effective protection of copyright works on an ongoing basis. Technology, even when robust and reliable, will attract hackers and pirates. Technical specifications, where possible, anticipate this contingency in order to maintain the effectiveness and robustness of the measure used. Technological measures are to be designed to be as tamper resistant as possible and, where possible, appropriate procedures put into place to recover swiftly and effectively from an unlawful breach of the system.

At the same time, technological measures are needed to be implemented in ways that do not impose unreasonable costs or burdens on equipment manufacturers and service providers. Standard technological measures can provide effective protections of copyright without unnecessarily affecting the overall quality of the user experience. This can be accomplished by interfering with the image or sound, or by otherwise materially degrading the quality of the content and/or service, or the performance of the device.

VI. Chapter Summary

eCommerce initiatives impact information technology, people, processes, and organizational systems. A multidisciplinary and holistic perspective that addresses technological, business, and legal issues is necessary to address eCommerce challenges.

eCommerce technologies are the fundamental infrastructure for commerce, communication and communities in the information age. Basic advancements in engineering and computer technologies are spawning an astounding array of new applications that extends the use of computers and networking into all aspects of economic, social, and political life.

While the vision of a networked, information society is most compelling, the continuing process of technological developments and their applications poses a serious challenge to define research priorities that sufficiently address both the emerging vision of the future and the need to foster and impart basic scientific body of knowledge.

Assuring continued developments in eCommerce technologies have many overarching U.S. interests. Despite heightened interest and initiatives within the private sector, some fundamental components that enable efficient digital markets will be ignored if left to the private sector because there exist very few private incentives to pursue them. Public good, characteristics of networks, information, digital products, and the peculiarities of space less, contactless markets bring about potential market failures. These factors demand a more active role and leadership from the public sector such as governments and the stakeholders in the basic research community.

Research issues in eCommerce are not as clear-cut as they are currently perceived and treated by both public and scientific community. A single technology or an application applies to a diversity of individuals, industries, and organizations and is used for many disparate purposes. Privacy and security issues, for example, have wider implications that cannot be adequately dealt with by technical solutions. Nevertheless, existing research efforts are largely fragmented rather than integrated within multidisciplinary frameworks, resulting in narrowly focused projects that seldom take into account the broader implications of eCommerce in related applications, economic efficiency, and social organizations.

Furthermore, eCommerce technologies are tools, i.e., an infrastructure that enables new types of organizations, relationships, and market mechanisms. Technological developments affecting the society as a whole will challenge basic assumptions and models in economic and social sciences, bringing about the need for systematic research activities to generate knowledge and methods needed to maximize their potential. As effective technologies mature and commercial applications expand into all economic and social activities, their implications will no longer remain either commercial or technical. Firms will organize and operate differently; consumer-producer relationships will change; new products and services will be transacted under new types of market arrangements. Changes in turn demand new technologies and applications to address new and unanticipated needs. Traditional models and theories are built from experiences in physical economy while the networked, computer-aided electronic environment differs fundamentally from physical markets.

Although computer and engineering sciences have laid the foundation for the digital economy, future developments cannot be made efficient if basic understanding of how technologies impact the economy or the society is lacking. A focused and increased level of interest of government and funding by the research organizations is critical in fermenting new knowledge and promoting basic scientific understanding of the implications of eCommerce.

VII. Project Demonstrating Excellence Summary

Intellectual property rights play an increasingly important role in economic and technological development and cultural expression. With the advent and exponential growth of the Internet, these rights are subject to an unprecedented global assault, threatening the value of those rights to public, industries, and governments. The global nature of the Internet presents unique challenges to a predictable, minimalist environment in which eCommerce can flourish. The stakes are high in terms of both economics and ideology. A significant discussion of these issues has occurred among stakeholder groups, in the U.S. Congress and in the entertainment industry. The copyright challenges between the entertainment industry and the public underscores why U.S. Congress and the courts must protect all stakeholders to exercise their rights.

Widespread piracy stifles commercial and academic creativity and inventiveness, and discourages the dissemination of products and services protected as intellectual property. There is a critical need for an enactment of adequate and effective domestic and foreign intellectual property laws that protect the rights of intellectual property owners and allow for the vigorous enforcement of those rights. The laws should acknowledge the rights of creators and owners of IP products and services; comply with the international standards for the protection and set penalties to deter infringement. Providing an appropriate level of access to IP copyright is critical to realizing the promise of the information age. Ensuring that this appropriate level of access becomes a reality raises a number of difficult issues that in the aggregate constitute the impact on eCommerce. This study articulated these difficult issues, provided a framework for thinking about them and offered ways of moving towards a resolution.

Intellectual property has a tremendous impact on eCommerce and society, resulting in a corresponding diversity of interests, motivations, and values. Some stakeholders see the issues in economic terms; some in philosophical terms; others in technological terms; and still others in legal, ethical, or social policy terms. There are also a variety of important forces at work-regulations, markets, social norms, and technology-all of which must be considered and all of which may also be used in dealing with the issues. Knowing about the full range of forces may open up additional routes for dealing with issues; not every problem need be legislated into submission. Individuals exploring these issues are well advised to be cognizant of all the forces at work to avoid being blind-sided by any of them; to avail themselves of the opportunity to use any of the forces when appropriate; to be aware of the process by which each of them comes about; and to consider the degree of public scrutiny of the values embedded in each.

The first two chapters of this study focused on the implications for business, society, and individuals that arise from the everyday use of the information infrastructure with an emphasis on intellectual property copyright that has been published in the traditional sense. The next two chapters addressed research methodology, data collected, and analyzed for actions that can be initiated to help in getting beyond the current impact on IP copyright. The last chapter offered interpretation, conclusions, and suggestions for further research for the formulation of appropriate public policy and copyright law.

One of the key contributions of this study is to urge an appropriate IP copyright framework for use by the research community and policy makers, one that acknowledges the full spectrum of stakeholders and forces. A significant portion of this study may be viewed as promising research expressing a range of perspectives on controversial IP copyright issues and the evolution of eBusiness models. For those issues, a summary of alternative perspectives is provided with the intent of exposing the core issues to aid future research.

This study also suggests a caution to policy makers to contemplate changes to law or policy with the utmost care.

Intellectual property copyright will surely flourish in the information age. It is clear, however, that major adaptations will have to take place to ensure sufficient protection for content creators and rights holders, thereby helping to ensure that an extensive and diverse supply of IP is available to the public. Major adaptations will also be needed to ensure that the important public purposes embodied in copyright law, such as public access, are fulfilled in the digital context. Considering the promise of the study, the author of the Project Demonstrating Excellence is optimistic that viable Intellectual property copyright solutions will be realized in near future for successful global eCommerce transactions.

APPENDIX – A

REFERENCES

REFERENCES

Acken, J. M. (1998). "How Watermarking Adds Value to Digital Content," *Communications of the ACM,* 41(7):75-77.

Adler, P. & P. (1987) *Membership Roles in Field Research.* Beverly Hills: Sage.

Angeles, R. (2000), "Revisiting the role of Internet-EDI in the current electronic commerce scene", <u>Logistics Information Management,</u> Vol 13 Issue 1, MCB

Aoki, K (1998a). "Considering multiple and overlapping sovereignties: Liberalism, libertarianism, national sovereignty, "Global" intellectual property, and the Internet," *Indiana Journal of Global Legal Studies,* volume 5, number 2, at <u>http://ijgls.indiana.edu/archive/05/02/aoki.shtml,</u> accessed 7 January 2002.

Aoki, K. (1998b). "Neocolonialism, anticommons property, and biopiracy in the (not-so-brave) new world order of international intellectual property protection," *Indiana Journal of Global Legal Studies,* volume 6, number 1, at <u>http://ijgls.indiana.edu/archive/06/01/aoki.shtml,</u> accessed 7 January 2002.

Archer N. and Yuan Y. (2000), "Managing business-to-business relationships throughout the e-commerce procurement life cycle", <u>Internet Research: Electronic Networking Applications and Policy,</u> Vol 10 Issue 5, MCB

ARL (1998). *Digital Millenium Copyright Act.* Retrieved May 19, 2001, <u>http://www.arl.org/info/frn/copy/dmca.html</u> and <u>http://hrrc.org/html/dmca-leg-hist.html</u>

ARL (2002). *Time Line: A History of Copyright in the United States.* Retrieved June 21, 2002, <u>http://arl.cni.org./info/frn/copy/timeline.html</u>

Bamfield J. (1994), "Learning by Doing: Electronic Data Interchange Adoption by Retailers", <u>Logistics Information Management,</u> Vol 07 Issue 6, MCB

Barlow, J.P.(1996). "Selling wine without bottles: The economy of mind on the global net," In: Lynn Hershman-Leeson (editor). *Clicking in: Hot links to a digital culture,* Seattle: Bay Press, pp. 148-172. Also appeared as J.P. Barlow, 1994, "Economy of ideas: A framework for patents and copyrights in the Digital Age" *Wired,* volume 2, number 3 (March), pp.84-90, 126-129, at <u>http://www.wired.com/wired/archive/2.03/economy.ideas_pr.html,</u> Retrieved January 8, 2002.

Benko, Robert P. (1987). <u>Protecting Intellectual Property Rights: Issues and Controversies.</u> Washington, D.C.: American Enterprise Institute for Public Policy Research.

Berg, B. (1989) *Qualitative Research Methods for the Social Sciences.* Boston: Allyn & Bacon.

Berelson, B. (1952). *Content Analysis in Communication Research.* Glencoe, Ill: Free Press.

Bergman, Marilyn. "*Copyright Order Belongs on the Cyber-Frontier.*" <u>Billboard</u> 11 Oct. 1997: 10+. Retrieved February 18, 2002, <u>http://www.billboard.com/billboard/index.jsp</u>

Bhatt G.D. (2001), "Business process improvement through electronic data interchange (EDI) systems: an empirical study", <u>Supply Chain Management: An International Journal</u>, Vol 6 Issue 2, MCB

Bhatt G.D. and Emdad A.F. (2001), "An analysis of the virtual value chain in electronic commerce", <u>Logistics Information Management</u>, Vol 14 Issue 1/2, MCB
Bhatt G.D. (2000), "Exploring the relationship between information technology, infrastructure and business process re-engineering", <u>Business Process Management Journal</u>, Vol 06 Issue 2, MCB

Bonisteel S. (2001), "Update: One Quarter Of Firms Will Bill B2B Online By 2002. (Industry Trend or Event)", <u>Newsbytes News Network</u>, Feb 20, 2001

Bons, R.W.H., Lee, R.M., & Wagenaar, R.W. (1998). Designing trustworthy interorganizational trade procedures for open electronic commerce, *International Journal of Electronic Commerce*, 2(3).

Bontis N. and Castro A.D. (2000), "The First World Congress on the Management of Electronic Commerce: review and commentary", <u>Internet Research: Electronic Networking Applications and Policy</u>, Vol 10 Issue 5, MCB

Cate, F.H. (1998). "Introduction: Sovereignty and the globalization of intellectual property," *Indiana Journal of Global Legal Studies,* volume 6, number 1, at <u>http://ijgls.indiana.edu/archive/06/01/cate.shtml</u>, Retrieved January 11, 2002.

Chan C. and Swatman P.M.C. (2000), "From EDI to Internet commerce: the BHP Steel experience", <u>Internet Research: Electronic Networking Applications and Policy</u>, Vol 10, MCB

Clark, D. (2002). *How Copyright Became Controversial.* National Journal's Technology Daily. Retrieved June 15, 2002, <u>http://www.cfp2002.org/proceedings/proceedings/clark.pdf</u>

Clarke, R. (2000). *Appropriate Research Methods for Electronic Commerce.* Retrieved March 22, 2002, <u>http://www.anu.edu.au/people/Roger.Clarke/EC/ResMeth.html</u>

Creswell, J.W. (1998). Qualitative inquiry and research design: Choosing among five traditions. Thousand Oaks, CA: Sage.

Crews, K.D. (1998). "Harmonization and the goals of copyright: Property rights or cultural progress?" *Indiana Journal of Global Legal Studies,* volume 6, number 1, at <u>http://ijgls.indiana.edu/archive/06/01/crews.shtml</u>, January 10, 2002.

Committee on Intellectual Property Rights in the Emerging Information Infrastructure, National Research Council. (2000). *The Digital Dilemma: Intellectual Property in the Information Age.* National Academy Press.

Cunningham, M. (2000). *How to Build a Profitable E-Commerce Strategy.* Perseus Publishing Cabridge Massachusetts.

CyberAtlas. (2002). *Big Boosts in Broadband.* Retrieved May 20, 2002, http://cyberatlas.internet.com/markets/broadband/article/0,,10099_1141701,00.html#table1

Deitel, H; Deitel, P; Steinbuhler, K (2001). *e-Business and e-Commerce for Managers*. Prentice Hall, Upper Saddle River, NJ.

Delong, J.V. (2002). *Defending Intellectual Property*. Project on Technology & Innovation. Competitive Enterprise Institute, Washington. Retrieved May 15, 2002., http://www.cei.org/pdf/2368.pdf

Dhillon G. and Caldeira M. (2000), "Interpreting the adoption and use of EDI in the Portuguese clothing and textile industry", Information Management & Computer Security, Vol 8 Issue 4, MCB.

Drahos, P. (1997). "States and intellectual property: The past, the present and the future," In D. Saunders and B. Sherman (editors). *From Berne to Geneva: Recent developments in international copyright and neighbouring rights*. Brisbane: Griffith University, Australian Key Centre for Cultural and Media Policy.

Drummond R. (2000), "XML: What's Still Needed for B2B? (Industry Trend or Event)", e-Business Advisor, May 2000 v18 i5 p44.

eCommerce Statistics. (2002). *Statistics for Electronic Transactions*. Retrieved July 25, 2002, http://www.epaynews.com/statistics/transactions.html

Edwards P. (2001), "IDC Predicts a Boom, Not Gloom for Asia's B2B eCommerce Markets", Retrieved April 23, 2001, http://www.idc.com

Eisner, E.W. (1998). *The enlightened eye: Qualitative inquiry and the enhancement of educational practise*. Upper Saddle River, NJ: Prentice Hall.

Esteve, P.R., Schuknecht, L. (1999). *A Quantitative Assessment of Electronic Commerce*. Economic Research and Analysis Division (ERAD)/ / World Trade Organization. Retrieved March 14, 2002, http://netec.mcc.ac.uk/BibEc/data/Papers/fthwtoera99-01.html

Fedorowicz, J. & Konsynski, B. (1992) Organizational support systems: bridging business and decision processes, *Journal of Management Information Systems*, 8(4), 5-25.

Fiedler U. et al (1999), "Quality of Service in Business-to-Business E-Commerce Applications", 1060-9857-99, 1999, IEEE.

Fisher M. (2000), "Using e-commerce to deliver high productivity", Work Study, Vol 49 Issue 2, MCB

Fraser J. et al (2000), "The strategic challenge of electronic commerce", Supply Chain Management: An International Journal, Vol 05 Issue 1, MCB

Fridman S. (2000), "B2B E-commerce To Become More Global - Gartner 02/17/00. (Industry Trend or Event)", Newsbytes, Feb 17, 2000 pNA

Garnett, Nic. *"WIPO to have Profound Effect on Music."* Billboard 18 Jan. 1997: 6+. Retrieved, February, 18, 2001, http://www.billboard.com/billboard/index.jsp

Gartner-Dataquest. (2002). *Twenty-Five Years, One Billion PCs*. Retrieved June 28, 2002, http://cyberatlas.internet.com/big_picture/hardware/article/0,,5921_1380441,00.html

Gattiker U.E. (2000), "Using the Internet for B2B activities: a review and future directions for research", Internet Research: Electronic Networking Applications and Policy, Vol 10 Issue 2, MCB

Geller, P.E. (1998). "From patchwork to network: Strategies for international intellectual property in flux," at http://www-rcf.usc.edu/~pgeller/patchnet.htm, accessed 9 January 2002. Also P.E. Geller, 1998, "From patchwork to network: Strategies for international intellectual property in flux," *Duke Journal of Comparative and International Law,* volume 9, number 1 (Fall), pp. 69-90.

General Accounting Office, U.S. (1996). *Content Analysis: A Methodology for Structuring and Analyzing Written Material.* GAO/PEMD-10.3.1. Washington, D.C.

Graham G. and Hardaker G. (2000), "Supply-chain management across the Internet", International Journal of Physical Distribution & Logistics Management, Vol 30 Issue 3/4, MCB

Griffiths J. et al (2001), "A customer-supplier interaction model to improve customer focus in turbulent markets", Managing Service Quality, Vol 11 Issue 1, MCB

Haag, S; Cummings, M; McCubbrey, D. (2002). Management Information Systems for the Information Age (3rd ed.). McGraw-Hill Irvin.

Hagel III, J; Armstrong, A. (1997). *Net Gain – expanding markets through virtual communities*. Harvard Business School Press.

Halhead R. (1995), "Breaking down the barriers to free information exchange", Logistics Information Management, Vol 08 Issue 1, MCB

Hammant J. (1995), "Information technology trends in logistics", Logistics Information Management, Vol 08 Issue 6, MCB

Han S. (1997), "A conceptual framework of the impact of technology on customer-supplier relationships", Journal of Business & Industrial Marketing, Vol 12 Issue 1, MCB

Hanson, W. (2002). *Principles of Internet Marketing*. South-Western College Publishing. Thomson Learning.

Hardy, T. (1998). *Project Looking Forward - Sketching the Future of Copyright in a Network World*. U.S. Copyright Office Report. Retrieved February 10, 2002, (http://www.copyright.gov/docs/thardy.pd.)

Hoffman, D. L; Novak, T.P. (2000). *Bridging the Digital Divide: The Impact of Race on Computer Access and Internet Use*. Vanderbilt University. Retrieved January 16, 2002, http://www.observetory.com/digital.htm

Holland, Bill. (1997). *"Crucial Copyrights Bills Advance In House: Legislation Extends Term, Covers Theft Via Computer."* Billboard 11 Oct. 1997: 9+. Retrieved Februay 18, 2002, http://www.billboard.com/billboard/index.jsp

Holsti, O.R. (1969). *Content Analysis for the Social Sciences and Humanities*. Reading, MA: Addison-Wesley.

Howe, W. (2001). *A brief history of the Internet.* An anecdotal history of the people and communities that brought about the Internet and the Web. Retrieved March 18, 2002, (http://www.walthowe.com/navnet/history.html)

Hsieh C. and Lin B. (1998), "Internet commerce for small businesses", Industrial Management & Data Systems, Vol 98 Issue 3, MCB

Hsieh, Lilli, Jennifer M. McCarthy, Elizabeth Monkus (2001). "Intellectual Property Crimes." American Criminal Law Review 35.3: 899-942.

IITF 'White Paper' (1995). *Intellectual Property and the National Information Infrastructure. The Report of the Working Group on Intellectual Property Rights.* Retrieved January 20, 2002, http://www.uspto.gov/web/offices/com/doc/ipnii/

Intellectual Property Law Server (2002). *Intellectual Property Survey.* Retrieved July 9, 2002, http://www.intelproplaw.com/?survey?survey

Internet Mergers and Acquisition. (2002). *First Half Report: Internet M&A Spending Up in Q2, but Down from 2001 Levels.* Retrieved June 30, 2002, http://www.webmergers.com/editorial/article.php?id=57

Internet Society, 2002. *A Brief History of the Internet and Related Networks.* Retrieved March 11th, 2002, http://www.isoc.org/internet/history/brief.shtml

Jelassi, T. & Figon, O. (1994). Competing through EDI at Brun Passot: achievements in France and ambitions for the single European market. *MIS Quarterly,* 18(4), 337-352.

Kalokota, R and Robinson, M. (2001). *e-Business, 2.0 roadmap for success* (2nd.). Addison-Wesley.

Kalakota, R., & Whinston, A. (1997). *Electronic commerce: A manager's guide.* Reading, MA: Addison-Wesley.

Kappelman L.A. et al (1996), "A manager's guide to electronic data interchange: doing business on the information superhighway", Logistics Information Management, Vol 9 Issue 1, MCB

Keeffe M.O. (2001), "Myths and realities of e-commerce in the perishable foods industries: unleashing the power of reputation and relationship assets", Supply Chain Management: An International Journal, Vol 6 Issue 1

Kim, B; Barua, A; Whinston, A. (2001). "Virtual field experiements for a digital economy: a new research methodology for exploring an information economy", Decision Support Systems 32 (2002) 215-231.

King J. (1999), "Studies see soaring B2B e-commerce. (Industry Trend or Event)", <u>Network World</u>, Dec 27, 1999 pNA

Koh S.C. et al (2000), "Measuring uncertainties in MRP environments", <u>Logistics Information Management</u>, Vol 13 Issue 3, MCB

Krippendorff, K. (1980). *Content Analysis: An Introduction to Its Methodology*. Newbury Park, CA: Sage.

Lankford W.M. and Johnson J.E. (2000), "EDI via the Internet", <u>Information Management & Computer Security</u>, Vol 08 Issue 1, MCB

Lauer, J.M., & Asher, J.W. (1998). *Composition research: Empirical designs*. New York: Oxford University Press.

Lau K. (2000), Director of Information Technology Services, speech at a management symposium on the challenges and opportunities of e-management today (May 26 2000) http://www.info.gov.hk/gia/general/200005/26/0526113.htm

Leedy, P.D. & Ormord, J.E. (2001). Practical Research: Planning and Design. Merrill Prentice Hall.

Leith, P. (1997). "Book review of James Boyle's *Shamans, software and spleens: law and the construction of the Information Society*," *Journal of Information, Law and Technology* (JILT), 1997, number 2 (30 June), at <u>http://elj.warwick.ac.uk/jilt/bookrev/97_2leit/</u>, Retrieved January 12, 2002.

Lofland, J. & L. (1984) *Analyzing Social Settings*. Belmont, CA: Wadsworth.

Loebbecke C. and Schäfer S. (2001), "Web portfolio based electronic commerce: the case of transtec AG", <u>Logistics Information Management</u>, Vol 14 Issue 1/2, MCB

Loughlin P. (1999), "Viewpoint: E-commerce strengthens suppliers' position", <u>International Journal of Retail & Distribution Management</u>, Vol 27 Issue 2, MCB

Lucking-Reiley D. and Spulber D.F. (2000), "Business-to-business electronic commerce", <u>Journal of Economic Perspectives</u>.

Lucy, J., J. S., & Maher, D. (1997). "Music on the Internet and the Intellectual Property Protection Problem," pp. SS77-SS83 in *Proceedings of the International Symposium on Industrial Electronics*. New York: IEEE Computer Society Press.

McIvor R. et al (2000), "Electronic commerce: re-engineering the buyer-supplier interface", <u>Business Process Management Journal</u>, Vol 06 Issue 2, MCB

McNurlin, B; Sprague, R.(2002). *Information Systems Management In Practice* (5th edi.). NJ: Printice Hall Upper Saddle River.

Min H. and Galle W. P. (1999), "Electronic commerce usage in business-to-business purchasing", <u>International Journal of Operations & Production Management</u>, Vol 19 Issue 9, MCB

Nayyer, K. (2000). Globalization of Information: Intellectual Property Law Implications. First Monday, volume 7, number 1. URL: <u>http://firstmonday.org/issues/issue7_1/nayyer/index.html</u>

O'Brien, J. (2001). Introduction to Information Systems. Essentials for the Internetworked E-Business Enterprise (10th ed.). McGraw-Hill Irvin

OECD Report. (1999).*The Economic and Social Impact of Electronic Commerce.* Retrieved March 25, 2001, <u>http://www.oecd.org/EN/home/0,,EN-home-29-nodirectorate-no-no-no-29,00.html</u>

Peshkin, A. (1998). Understanding complexity: A gift of qualitative research. Anthropology and Education Quarterly, 19, 416-424.

Rappa, M. (2001). Business Models on the Web. Managing the Digital Enterprise. Retrieved January 17, 2002. <u>http://digitalenterprise.org/models/models.html</u>

Ratnasingam P. (2000), "The influence of power on trading partner trust in electronic commerce", <u>Internet Research: Electronic Networking Applications and Policy</u>, Vol 10 Issue 1, MCB

Ratnasingham P. (1998), "Internet-based EDI trust and security", <u>Information Management & Computer Security</u>, Vol 6 Issue 1, MCB

Robson L. (1994), "EDI – Changing Business Practice", <u>Logistics Information Management</u>, Vol 07 Issue 4, MCB

Roberts, C.W. (Ed.) (1997). *Text Analysis for the Social Sciences: Methods for Drawing Statistical Inferences from Texts and Transcripts.* Mahwah, NJ: Lawrence Erlbaum Associates.

Rosenberg, S.D., Schnurr, P.P., & Oxman, T.E. (1990). Content analysis: A comparison of manual and computerized systems. *Journal of Personality Assessment, 54* (1 & 2), 298-310.

Samuelson, P. (1999). "Intellectual Property and the Digital Economy: Why the Anti-Circumvention Regulations Need to Be Revised," 14 *Berkeley Technology Law Journal*, pp. 519-566.

Seideman, T. (1996) "What Sam Walton learned from the Berlin airlift," *Audacity: The Magazine of Business Experience*, Spring, 52-61.

Shapiro, C; Varian, H (1999): Information Rules*: A Strategic Guide for the Network Economy.* Harvard University Press.

Schwartz, David. (1999). <u>Strange Fixation: Bootleg Sound Recordings Enjoy the Benefits of Improving Technology</u>. Federal Communications Law Journal. 25 March 1999.

Skjoett-Larsen T. (2000), "European logistics beyond 2000", <u>International Journal of Physical Distribution & Logistics Management</u>, Vol 30 Issue 5, MCB

Stemler, S., and Bebell, D. (1998). *An Empirical Approach to Understanding and Analyzing the Mission Statements of Selected Educational Institutions*. Paper presented at the annual meeting of the New England Educational Research Organization. Portsmouth, New Hampshire. Available: ERIC Doc No. ED 442 202.

Survey.net, (2002). *Online Intellectual Property Survey. Property rights in cyberspace?* Retrieved January 22, 2002, <u>http://www.survey.net/sv-ip0.htm</u>

Trepper C. (2000), E-Commerce Strategies, Microsoft

Turban, E; Lee, J; King, D; Chung, H. (1999). *Electronic Commerce A Managerial Perspective*. Prentice Hall, Upper Saddle River, NJ.

U.S. Copyright Office. (2000). *Copyright Basics*. Retrieved June 25, 2002. <u>http://www.loc.gov/copyright/</u>

U.S. Department of Commerce. (2001). *U.S. Government E-Commerce Policy*. Retrieved June 2, 2001, <u>http://www.commerce.gov/Electronic_Commerce/</u>

Vijayasarathy L.R. and Tyler M.L. (1997), "Adoption factors and electronic data interchange use: a survey of retail companies", <u>International Journal of Retail & Distribution Management</u>, Vol 25 Issue 9, MCB

Walcott, H.F. (1994). *Transforming qualitative data: Description, analysis, and interpretation*. Thousand Oaks, CA: Sage.

Walton S.V. and Gapta J.N.D. (1999), "Electronic data interchange for process change in an integrated supply chain", <u>International Journal of Operations & Production Management</u>, Vol 19 Issue 4, MCB

Warkentin M. et al (2001), "E-knowledge networks for inter-organizational collaborative e-business", <u>Logistics Information Management</u>, Vol 14 Issue 1/2, MCB

Weber, R. P. (1990). *Basic Content Analysis*, 2nd ed. Newbury Park, CA.

Wheelock, A., Haney, W., & Bebell, D. (2000). What can student drawings tell us about high-stakes testing in Massachusetts? *TCRecord.org*. Available: <u>http://www.tcrecord.org/Content.asp?ContentID=10634</u>.

WIPO, (2000). *Electronic Commerce and Intellectual Property*. World Intellectual Property Organization. Retrieved March 15, 2001, <u>http://www.wipo.org/about-ip/en/</u>

Wired News.(1999). *RIAA Sets the Record Straight*. Wired Digital Inc. Retrieved March 26, 2002, <u>http://www.wired.com/news/news/culture/mpthree/story/18693.html</u>.

WTO, (1998). *Work Programme on Electronic Commerce.* Retrieved December 17, 2001, http://www.wto.org/english/tratop_e/ecom_e/wkprog_e.htm

Zwass, V. (1996). Electronic commerce: structures and issues, *International Journal of Electronic Commerce,* 1(1), 3-23.

APPENDIX – B

SURVEY CONSENT FORM

Informed Consent Form

Research with Human Subjects

Survey#1

Source: http://www.survey.net/sv-ip0.htm

Your confidentiality is assured, survey responses are anonymous. We appreciate your honest answers to the questions below.

Online Intellectual Property Survey

What do you think about property rights in cyberspace?

1. **What is your age?**

2. **Your Sex:**

3. **Your highest level of education completed:**

4. **Have you ever done any of the following:** *(check all that apply)*

 ☐ - downloaded an image off the internet - not knowing if it was copyrighted

 ☐ - downloaded an image off the internet that was copyrighted

 ☐ - downloaded a MIDI file of a popular song without paying a fee

 ☐ - downloaded a MP3 file of a popular song without paying a fee

 ☐ - built a web page using images or content from another web site without permission

 ☐ - transferred a copyrighted file via ICQ

 ☐ - burned an unauthorized cd containing copyrighted material

 ☐ - let a friend borrow your program disks to install software

 ☐ - let a friend borrow an audio cd/tape to make a copy

5. **Have you ever bought an album/cd that you first heard about after obtaining an illegal digital copy?**

   | No Answer ▼ |

6. **Have you ever purchased a software title after originally obtaining an unauthorized/pirated copy?**

   | No Answer ▼ |

7. **have you ever obtained a commercial software program from the net without paying for it?**

   | No Answer ▼ |

8. **have you ever registered or "cracked" a program with an unauthorized key or serial number?**

   | No Answer ▼ |

9. **Do you use any of the following software?** *(check all that apply)*

   ☐ - Napster
   ☐ - Winamp
   ☐ - MusicMatch Jukebox
   ☐ - Microsoft Media Player
   ☐ - Quicktime
   ☐ - Online mp3 search engines
   ☐ - IRC DCC
   ☐ - ICQ

10. Do you think web pages should be copyrighted and protected
    as intellectual property?

11. Do you believe digital IMAGE files should be afforded the
    same protections in cyberspace as their offline couterparts?

12. Do you believe digital AUDIO files should be afforded the same
    protections in cyberspace as their offline couterparts?

13. Do you have any copyrighted material (images, audio files,
    software, or other data) that you downloaded from the net to
    your hard drive without specific permission?

14. Do you have any copyrighted material (images, audio files,
    software, or other data) installed on your machine without a
    legitimate license?

15. Do you think companies that produce software such as Napster
    should be held responsible in one form or another for the
    illegal activities (piracy of copyrighted material) their software

may facilitate?

> No Answer ▼

16. **Do you think there is a difference between software such as Napster, which helps people download MP3s regardless of whether they're copyrighted, and e-mail, usenet or other programs which afford similar abilities to acquire copyrighted material?**

> No Answer ▼

17. **How would you rule in a case where an artist is suing a company that makes a program that facilitates easy copying of their material without remuneration?**

> No Answer

S O U N D - O F F - Your opinion matters!

- **Please share your thoughts regarding online intellectual property issues:**

  (*Limit this to one or two sentences*)

Thanks very much for participating in the survey!

To submit your survey choices, select:

or [Reset survey settings]

You can view the latest survey results after you submit your answers.

Please note that you should only complete each survey <u>once</u>.

Your source for information, opinions & demographics from the

Net Community!

Survey-Net is *the* **source for user demographics on the Internet. We invite everyone to participate in our online surveys -** the first of their kind **where you can instantly see the compiled results! The information accumulated online is available to everyone on the net. You are free to republish/use any portion of our survey results as long as we are acknowledged.**

Copyright ©1994-2000, [   ]/InterCommerce Corporation,

All rights reserved worldwide

Send comments to *<u>Survey.Net</u>*

Survey#2

Welcome to the intellectual property law server at
www.intelproplaw.com

Terms of Use

Before you Use this Website
You Must Agree to Assume All Risks and Losses Resulting Directly or Indirectly from
its Use. This website is intended to be a resource for professionals.

Source: http://www.intelproplaw.com/?survey

Intellectual Property Survey

**Should tools that make it very easy to
breach copyright be illegal even
though there may be some other
legitimate use for those tools?**

C Yes

C No

C Don't Know

Feel free to contact at
webmaster@intelproplaw.com.
iKnight Technologies Inc.